PROVENÇAL
COOKING

PROVENÇAL

COOKING

Savoring the Simple Life in France

MARY ANN CAWS

Drawings by Clive Blackmore

PEGASUS BOOKS

NEW YORK

PROVENÇAL COOKING
SAVORING THE SIMPLE LIFE IN FRANCE

PEGASUS BOOKS LLC
45 WALL STREET, SUITE 1021
NEW YORK, NY 10005

COPYRIGHT © 2008 BY MARY ANN CAWS

ILLUSTRATION COPYRIGHT © 2008 CLIVE BLACKMORE

FIRST PEGASUS BOOKS EDITION 2008

Interior design by Maria Fernandez

LIBRARY OF CONGRESS CATALOGING-IN-PUBLICATION DATA IS AVAILABLE.

ISBN: 978-1-60598-020-1

10 9 8 7 8 6 5 4 3 2 1

PRINTED IN THE UNITED STATES OF AMERICA
DISTRIBUTED BY W. W. NORTON & COMPANY, INC.
WWW.PEGASUSBOOKS.US

My thanks for so many things to so many friends surrounding the Cabanon Biska. To all of them, this book of
memories and ongoing living is dedicated.

All the poems included here are by René Char, in my
translations—some are found in the New Directions
volume of his *Selected Poems,* edited by Mary Ann Caws
and Tina Jolas (New York, 1992). My thanks to New
Directions for permission to use them here.

I want to thank also my agent, Katherine Fausset, for her
ingenuity, and my editor, Jessica Case, for her enthusiasm;
the many friends and neighbors who contributed recipes;
my family; and my husband, Boyce Bennett.

Long Live . . .

> *This country is only a wish of the spirit,*
> *a counter-sepulchre.*

In my country, tender proofs of spring and badly-dressed
  birds are preferred to far-off goals.

Truth waits for dawn beside a candle. Window-glass is
  neglected. To the watchful, what does it matter?

In my country, we don't question a person deeply
  moved.

There is no malignant shadow on the capsized boat.

A cool greeting is unknown in my country.

We borrow only what can be returned increased.

There are leaves, many leaves, on the trees of my country.
  The branches are free to bear no fruit.

We don't believe in the good faith of the victor.

In my country, we say thank you.

CONTENTS

PROVENÇAL

COOKING

MEALS UNDER THE
MULBERRY TREE

It was to the table up the hill that I would bring my occasional visitors, it was under the mulberry tree overlooking a vineyard and a mountain that we'd chat over the events in our little village. How one simple grocery store had driven the other out of business. How the mountain was being developed, badly, but how, so far, our nearby hill had not much changed. How the rival factions for the mayor had waged their war, fighting over details.

Meals under the mulberry tree would always be punctuated by children, visiting and native, running in and out of the houses across the way, taking care of ducks, rabbits, and each other. We would be having some fragrant dish cooked on the grill outside, while Alexander's distinctive tenor voice would float out from the large ochre-colored house, with its Italian terra-cotta bouquet of fruit sculpted above the door.

Tonight we are ten for dinner, and we watch the mountain growing greener, and then darker purple, framed by the olive trees. Just when it is growing dark, and we have tasted Malcolm's new wine, Janet brings out of the kitchen across the road some perfectly ripe melons with strong-flavored mountain ham, and we are having Malcolm's **Gigot d'agneau/Grilled Lamb**.

Much later, after the salad and selection of goat cheeses, Janet brings out an old oval dish of *grès* pottery, filled with golden apricots and cream, sprinkled with lemon juice and sugar, and baked in a slow oven until they have wrinkled just slightly. We all add a dash of Grand Marnier from the bottle on the table, and fall silent.

I trudge back down the hill, happy. Never mind that I have to clear out the blackberry bushes tomorrow, with those roots that reach over and take hold everywhere, never mind that my back hurts, that the olive grove has gone, like my ivy. How lucky we all are.

HOW IT CAME ABOUT

L ife in the Vaucluse proceeds generally at a slow pace, dappled with the light and shade of the over hanging foliage and the mountains. We don't feel rushed, except to get the freshly baked bread in the morning before the *boulangerie* closes at noon, or to take the gas bottles down the hill before it is time to cook supper. This rhythm is the very opposite of what I used to think I wanted to live by. Growing up in the semi-deep South of the United States, where life always moved slowly and often seemed to drag, I wanted to be somewhere else more than anything. And I determined that when I was of deciding age, I would be part of a more rapid way of living. That has all changed in much of my life, as will be apparent in these pages.

I went to college at Bryn Mawr, and promptly fell in love with French literature. For the class entitled Baby French, our instructor instantly sidestepped all the usual chatter about hotel rooms and restaurants, and taught the present tense by imagining a panther leaping out from under the desk, closely followed by a reading of Rimbaud's dizzyingly brief poem "À une raison." I never figured exactly why we were saluting something so abstract as "a reason," nor what the reason was. It all remained peculiar and mysterious. Nor can I remember the poem, only that it will be forever intertwined with the panther in my mind. Thanks to that speedy training, I was allowed to go off to Paris for my junior year, Paris, where things and people and everything around seemed intense to me—intense and rapid.

That year, I did everything I could, visiting Rome with a gallant Frenchman, bicycling around Brittany, sleeping out all night on the tip of the Isle de la Cité in Paris and right outside the old monastery at Vézelay. In Paris, I studied piano with a student from the Conservatoire and practiced for long hours in my French home on the rue du Général Foy, in the chic 8th arrondissement, in a white high-ceilinged room with ornate gold trim and glass doors. I attended a series of superb and inexpensive concerts with a pass from the *Jeunesses Musicales de France,* hearing the great pianists Brendel and Backhaus and Kemp, and went to many half-understandable plays, including the opening performance of Beckett's *En Attendant Godot,* received without a great deal of warmth by the French public.

I muddled my way through a year-long lecture course at the political science branch of the Université de Paris called "Sciences Politiques" or "Sciences Po," where I disgraced myself in the final oral exam with a crowd of auditors sitting around in amusement, by getting Alexis de Tocqueville's dates exactly 200 years off. I went to weekly lectures on "*Le Culte du moi,*" or "The religion of me," having to do with Montaigne, Gide, and the differences between egotism and egoism. It ended with a six-hour written exam consisting of one question which I cannot remember now, despite the excitement of reflecting upon it for the very long moment. Required by Bryn Mawr to take a philosophy course, I chose one promising to deal with "modern philosophy," at l'Institut Catholique on the rue d'Assas. It always began with a five-minute Latin invocation, for which we stood with heads bowed, and of which I understood not a word. For the final exam, the very kind Benedictine father queried me about the distinction between some ritual and "our mass." Alas, I said, Father, I am not a Catholic, so I don't really know. He smiled indulgently, and that was that for philosophy that year. I was far more interested in a fellow student with a cleft in his chin and warm brown eyes who engaged me in the issue of who had knelt to whom at Canossa, at the meeting of Pope and Emperor. Of the answer I was uncertain, but knew above all that I loved France. Everything had a shape and a style there, and it was all quick.

When I returned to Bryn Mawr, things seemed different. Philosophy courses dealt with Boethius and Bishop Berkeley. Samuel Claggett Chew, a famous white-bearded sage, taught the Bible course enlivened with the apocrypha. My English course concerned Henry James, whose great *Golden Bowl* I read in a tree by the library, while two brilliant French professors, René Girard and Mario Maurin, taught us to read André Malraux, his novels and art criticism, and then the correspondence between Paul Claudel and André Gide—the former hard as a boulder, the latter bending like the proverbial and Pascalian reed. Irresistible.

After graduating from Bryn Mawr, I headed off for Yale to study with Victor Brombert and Henri Peyre, and met an English philosophy student named Peter, a name I had always loved. We were married in the very small Dwight Chapel, had a reception in the Hall of Graduate Studies, with toasts in Latin and Greek by our fellow students, and then left New Haven for universities in Michigan and Kansas before gravitating to New York life, Peter as an official of the Carnegie Corporation and then a philosophy professor, and I teaching French at Sarah Lawrence, then at Hunter College and the Graduate School of CUNY.

When the children came—a girl and a boy—we found they fit perfectly in the little plaid seats on the back of our bicycles for rides around Central Park. They rapidly became bilingual from their studies at the Lycée Français and our sabbatical leaves and summers spent in France. There they attended French schools, the Lycée Montaigne for our daughter Hilary ("But there is no woman saint named Hilary," the tight-laced French authorities protested), and a *collège* near the rue de L'Epée de Bois for Matthew, younger by two years. Nearby lived our friend the writer Edmond Jabès, so, more and more, France began to feel like home. In the summers, we would send the children to "La Poussinière," a camp in Normandy's Cabourg, a town celebrated as Proust's "Balbec," and they would return in their little red and blue outfits, bewildered and joyous.

LIFE IN THE
CABANON

As a family, we had always traveled a great deal in France. Living in Paris, we would make our way to Brittany in our yellow 2CV, or just tootle around in the forests of Fontainebleau and Rambouillet. Very unlike Manhattan it was, to say the least, and we felt, in our French times, very unlike New Yorkers. Not that we felt particularly rural either. To find any dwelling place in France would be hard, the dollar at that time being very low indeed in relation to the French currency. The sheets we were preserving from our Paris sabbatical were blue, the color of the sky we had been longing for all year, as we were sunk in the Paris gray. We thought of the blue skies, the dazzling light, and the lavender fields of Provence, and the idea did not go away.

Nor did we. I knew how sheets mattered. I remembered how Virginia Woolf, upon realizing she and Leonard could never live in the little port town of Cassis, where they had thought of buying a house, had thought first about who could best use the sheets they would be leaving behind. We could best use our own sheets, we thought.

It felt as if the things that mattered in France mattered

differently. If you didn't speak the language fluently, but cared about its art and literature, that was the crucial element. We cared, but we didn't have much in the way of French currency. But we had a kind of faith in Provence, and in its skies. One day we saw in a newspaper the following words, which seemed tinged with a sort of magic: VALLÉE DU VENTOUX. BASTIDON À AMÉNAGER. EAU DE SOURCE. CERISIERS, OLIVIERS, AMANDIERS. "In the valley of the Ventoux, *Bastidon* to be restored. Water from a spring. Almond trees, cherry trees, olive trees." That description says a lot, but there was a lot it did not say; and whatever sort of dwelling the "*bastide*" might have been, the owners or agents had used the still smaller version of the term: "*bastidon.*" What was certain was that it was clearly and definitely going to need to be restored. In a major way. And that was to go on and on. . . .

When my family and I first came to see the "*cabanon,*" as the agent called this small abandoned structure, it was a discouraging sight. Three fourths of the roof tiles were missing. There was an up and a down, but no stairs between them. You had to take a circuitous route around the back. The agent told us that for a time, rival brothers had owned this place, wanting no communication with each other. There was an opening in the wall near the back, a kind of slot of a window, or *fenestron,* where the brother who lived upstairs could see the other one, should he come up the slope behind the cabanon. Later, it had been used as a stable by the owner, who would take his siesta upstairs while the horse rested downstairs, endowing the earth with what turned out to be twenty-four wheelbarrows full.

The floor and ceiling between up and down—what there was of it—was made of the wood from grape crates. There were small ovals in many planks, by which the heavy crates had been carried, and these were ideally suited for catching dust. Rain had clearly been pouring in through the broken chimney upstairs, through the roof, onto those boards, and would continue to do so. Very depressing.

But something about it captured the imagination of our family, both children and grownups. The cabanon, hidden behind almond and cherry trees, marked off by rosemary shrubs and by those dry stone walls that, according to the agent, were standing above the original Roman walls at their base, sat far up on the hill, but not quite at the top. If we walked a bit farther up, we could see the chapel, Notre-Dame-des-Anges, for which the hill is named. Just the way the cabanon was lost in its foliage, set back from the road, like the name of the chapel, suggested quiet and calm, and we said we would give it a try. We would try to see how to live in this cabanon and we would soon learn the kind of perseverance it would require.

It would require a lot, and it still does. Little by little, I gave up rapidity, both as quest and as an ideal. I was clearly wrong about disliking the slowness of such a place. It is part of how we live in Provence, and it may well be the best part.

BUYING A CABANON

To purchase anything anywhere, the best practice comes from already having done it. Surely, the next time we buy a cabanon, we will know better how to do it.

It goes something like this: you, the agent, and the seller spend two or three afternoons around a *pastis*—that sticky opaque licorice drink that is the favorite of the region— sizing each other up. I take lots of water in my *pastis,* and the agent took almost none—we were about to be a soft touch. In the final stages, all the parties meet with the notary, and the discussion of currency takes place for a short while. Then, suddenly, the phone is said to be ringing. It is for the notary, of course, who promptly exits. Now this is the point at which the agent smiles, meaning you are supposed to slip to the seller an envelope containing a certain amount as a bribe or under-the-table sum. This is so you will not have to declare it or pay taxes on it, and everyone agrees with the subterfuge. The notary comes back in, wreathed in smiles; his phone call must have gone well, and he gets his hefty percentage of the sale. You sign the endless papers, hand over the cash, and, leaving behind the agent and the notary, both in very good moods, go to lunch with the seller, everyone still wreathed in smiles.

An amazing lunch, to celebrate, with the kind of cooking that takes days, and melts away gloriously in your mouth, from the opening *tapenade* through the foie gras sauté and array of cheeses to the profiteroles and cognac. All problems chased away. What could there be to worry about?

Well, quite a bit, actually. After lunch, our concerns began about those missing roof tiles and floorboards, as well as concerns about the fact that the terrain surrounding our cabanon was not actually ours because the seller still owned it so long as the cherry trees were still alive. As a minor point, there was also no electricity and no water except from the picturesque spring, a little hard to rely upon, although we didn't know how hard. And at the time, we thought the idea of gas lamps very picturesque.

Romantic notions of an idyllic life die hard. We had much, much work to do. The first six summers, we seemed, all of us, to be building always. Removing the manure from our little kitchen, we put great slabs of red stone in its place. An immense *puits perdu* had to be dug to stand in place of a sewage tank, the upstairs floor had to be repaired, the walls had to be fixed, much cementing and plastering had to be done, with what seemed to be the whole neighborhood standing about, making a great circle of feet around us as we bent over our task. When one part was finished, a chorus would break out:

> *C'est pas comme ça qu'il fallait faire!*
> That's not the way you should have done it!

And no one told us before? But now they were telling us, all at once, with large grins. The process was then repeated, same silence, same grins, same teasing. This must have been the testing time, to see how we would adapt to the way of life here, when it just seemed like cementing and plastering: in any case, those two skills stay with you.

NEIGHBORS

When we first came to the cabanon, they were the ones who welcomed us daily; Jean-Marie, tiny in stature, with his keen brown eyes slightly crossed, wearing, as always, his red T-shirt, and Augusta, his wife, with a kind face and gray hair, who liked us immediately, as we liked her. She urged us to call her "Tata," as her children did. Jean-Marie was the one who brought over to us the first purple grapes of the season in a little bunch, and the first beans in a dull green heap; he took our children, Matthew and Hilary, to see baby wild boars, always calling to them from the path between his *mas* and our little cabanon:

"*Eh! Mathieu! Hilary! O là!*"

to let us know he was coming, both when he arrived for his *pastis* at eleven and for a tiny cup of strong coffee at three in the afternoon, after nap time. In the morning, I would pour a goodly dose of the clear licorice-tasting pastis in a tall glass, waiting until Jean-Marie would say:

"*ça suffit!*" enough!

Of course, I have learned that in principle, it is one fifth *pastis* to four fifths icy spring water. My neighbors, Serge— Jean-Marie's older son—and his wife Suzanne freeze their water in plastic bottles so that it drips out through the ice, but I have no room in my tiny refrigerator, and no way will a large plastic bottle fit into the minuscule freezer. I have to think small. Some days I could find sufficient ice cubes. I stick to the 1 x 4 ratio, and choose the pastis they prefer.... Good neighbors give good lessons.

One day Jean-Marie brought me a book by the Provençal poet Gabriel Mistral, without asking whether I could read Provençal, but the point was made. He knew I loved poetry, and the gesture mattered more than the language. We used to spend hours listening to Jean-Marie's anecdotes, all of us. *"Diable!"* (*"The Devil!"*) he would say, when we would attempt to tell him something, "Diable!" It served for good and bad, ordinary and extraordinary. He was the essence of our hill, named, like the chapel, Notre-Dame-des-Anges, where his father and forefathers had lived before him, in the grand shadow of the Mont Ventoux. Their life as grape-growers has not been easy. Until a few years ago, they had no fresh water except that from a cistern, difficult for the raising of their four children: Ghislaine, their daughter, and Serge, Alain, and Claude. At harvest time, Tata would have to feed all the workers, and continue to help with the harvest, as well as take care of the family. *"Ah, Marianne. Je suis si fatiguée."* No wonder she was, and always is, tired.

And now, from next door there began to appear, more and more frequently, the whole Conil family bearing gifts, from their farmhouse or *mas* next door, to our much smaller dwelling. Some green beans in a little pot, a jar of freshly put-up apricot jam, and, later in the summer, a bunch of the first grapes, dewy and purple. We had become part of the hill. That our cabanon was so much smaller than their dwellings was a good thing. It showed that we were very far from the proverbial rich Americans.

At night the gas lamps would splutter over our soup, and we would sink into sleep happy and exhausted. But all was not neighborliness and good company. For years, it seemed to us, the man owning the lot right next to ours would come to check it out, sometimes with his wife's silent and squint-eyed brothers. We too often looked at this lot, mostly stones and trees, which he might, or might not, sell. His opinions on the topic were, like the whole question of water rights, oddly surreptitious. Whatever we could pay, his price was always somewhat higher, and that went on for years. Needless to say, we never acquired the lot, so even now the menace of too-closeness hovers over the cabanon, huddled in the middle of vegetation and brambles.

OUR CABANON

The cabanon had always been called *Le Cabanon Bisqua*, in honor of one of the first owners, who were given to frequent complaining. The name comes from the *patois* verb for whining: *bisquer*. It also means to annoy. Tata says her mother would call the fountain by that name, *Bisqua*. This was in the time that the water from the spring would be rationed out by days and hours, and when some rights-holder would surreptitiously filch some of the water from the metal holder that contained it. Who could tell?

Complaining, *bisquer,* has always been thought of as a good preventive measure in this region, which is one of the poorer parts of France. You complain about the wind, the rain, the sun, the drought, the rifts made in the cherries by the rain, the high price of living, and the low price of selling cherries or anything you grow, and, of course, your work. Not to complain would be to tempt fate, which already seems to take little tempting. You would be likely to attract evil fortune for having nothing to lament, or for not lamenting it. Evil fortune might feel compelled to pay you a visit, as it would think things were progressing just a little too well.

There are indeed a great many things to lament in Provence, and more are being invented every day even as I write. Some are traditional, forming the mainstays of conversation around the peaches, yellow or white, at the grocery store. Winds, for example. The great north wind, the all-important mistral, *"purifiant"* and clarifying, is powerful enough to cause marriages to split apart, to give you a headache, and to sour the milk. But it clears everything off, and up. We say of a superb day, "Ah," of course, "it is after the mistral."

The south wind, or *sirocco,* the unhealthy wind, is likely to put everyone in a bad mood. Too much or too little sun, too much or too little rain ruins the grapes, the melons, the tomatoes. It is also customary to complain of the intrusions into the region by foreigners: Belgians, Germans, Swiss, Dutch, English, Americans, or Parisians, who were the "foreignest" of all, according to my Provençal neighbors. *Tout ça, c'est des étrangers, quoi.*

Étranger: a dreaded term. A foreigner does not know how to live in this region. A foreigner may worry about being taken for a fool. Or she may accept, instead, to be someone *en train d'apprendre* (still learning), and that's a good way to be. As for the French language, I like the way it fills your mouth as well as your mind, even when you remain awkward in the fine points of the practical. The same is true of the Provençal language, which I finally stopped trying to learn, thinking that living and language were to some extent identical. When we finally gave up on our oil lamps for something more modern, we summoned a kindly young electrician. He came up the walk, and, not wearing my glasses (can't see without them, can't walk with them), I kissed him on both his very young round cheeks, thinking him a close friend. I forget how many times you kiss people's cheeks in the Vaucluse—at least three for new acquaintances, four for friends, and five for relatives. It takes ages to leave and to arrive. Having made this initial unbelievable *gaffe*, what should I do when the electrician leaves? Well, I kissed the electrician goodbye too, and now all our lights work along the long path down to the road, and everywhere else too.

From time to time, a few new faces would move into the village, and they would be called, simply, "*les nouveaux achats,*" the new purchases. In time, they will have blended in and perhaps become "*vacanciers*" instead of "*étrangers.*" Better than being a foreigner forever. Eventually, in the tiny market of the town, when someone would ask if we are back "for vacation," I learned to smile instead of bristling and answering testily: "But we work here." Whatever work we might have been doing at the time, it was assuredly not the local kind—we were neither working in the fields nor in an office or restaurant. My husband was particularly admired, since he was doing the hardest part of the manual work, to which we all contributed: he dug the ditches, laid the tiles, and chased the rats from around his table where his books were piled. And still managed to remain a professor of philosophy.

OUR VILLAGE

Mormoiron, the name of the village we were to inhabit and love, lies between two other small villages, Villes-sur-Auzon and Mazan. All three are linked by history, tradition, and gossip. Villes-sur-Auzon, or "Villes" for short, is reached by a poplar-bordered road, with the trees so near that they seem to touch the cars. It is a lovely village, conscious of its history, with a central square that often resounds with music and laughter. The little church has a gaily-lit steeple, with a red light shining out mysteriously over the tiled orange roofs that surround the square. The bells ring every hour, twice, in case you didn't hear them the first time.

Very different is Mazan, the village we have to go through to get to Carpentras, the main town of the region, and it is far more formal in mood than either Villes or Mormoiron. Traditionally, in Mazan, the farmers always used to wear their jackets to work in the field, and the girls were called, said one neighbor, "*tomates*" instead of "*jupes.*" The historic importance of the village is double that of Villes or of Mormoiron, which may account for its traditional mode and formality. There are its Gallo-Roman tombs, and the fact that the Marquis de Sade's family lived here in the eigh teenth century. The more elegant of the two hotels prides itself on being the Sade family home. There is still an air of mystery clinging to the village, to its narrow streets, and to its church, where a friend and I recently witnessed the conclusion of a marriage celebration, from behind the altar. The tall groom, in a cadet's uniform from the one-year military service obligatory for young men, stood ramrod-straight in the church doorway. Beside him stood the bride, elegant in a tight-fitting, easy-flowing long dress with swags, facing into the light. As the well-wishers outside threw their packets of rice into the air in great swirls, the priest closed the door to the outside, and we remained in the dark cool interior, feeling privileged to have witnessed this fortunate event from such a vantage point.

In between Villes and Mazan lies our village, Mormoiron, which has always been informal and not particularly
conscious of class. Here, farmers and workers have always
mingled, or so said Jean-Marie. But the villagers pay great
attention to each other, and to each other's timing of
things. When you are about to spray your vines, you circle
once on your tractor slowly about the village before doing
so, and pretty soon all your neighbors go out to spray
theirs, feeling it must be the right time to spray. The sense
of community is as strong as the sense of envy. Envy that
your neighbor's crops are doing better than yours, for
instance.

Our village is profiled against a horizon of mountain
slopes, a typical Provençal village. Small houses cling to
the hill, and the church stands at the center. Now it has
only one grocery store, instead of the five it housed at
the turn of the century when its business was good.
Mormoiron was once rich from *garance,* the crimson dye
used by the Zouave soldiers—and familiar to many of us
from the great actress Arletty's name in the film *Les
Enfants du Paradis,* "Garance." This *rubia tinctorum sativa*
that made Mormoiron rich once was introduced into the
Comtat Venaissin by Jean Althen, born in 1709 in Persia,
who had worked on the similar substance *alizarine,* a natural red coloring found in Turkish Anatolia. Then Louis
XV asked him to use it near Lyon, but he failed in that

endeavor, and retired to Monteux, near Avignon, in 1756, in a place called "Les Paluds" (the marshes)—thus the present name: Althen-les-Paluds. Then *garance* was replaced by a chemical substance invented in Germany, inexpensive to manufacture. This happening undid the former wealth of the village. The stories about this fall circulate from generation to generation. Some are tragic, like that of the former grocery store owner, who hanged herself over the betrayal by her husband. There are tales of acquisition, of greed, of loss, of sustained anger. Tales of vineyards going broke, *"étrangers"* in the local *patois,* like Belgians (called "les gens du nord," the people from the North), English, Americans, and Parisians, buying up cabanons which longtime residents of the village have wanted for years, because permissions have been refused by the mayor, or else granted to the undeserving—read: foreigners with cash. There is always a great deal of complaining.

Four fifths of the Mormoiron population has moved away over the years, and, of those that remain, only twenty percent live in the village. The windows of the old houses have been filled in, for an age-old tax on each window is fierce. There is an air of erstwhileness about the place. Old-timers in the village will tell curious newcomers the difference between what was then and what is now. Collective memory is strong in the Vaucluse, as in all the rural areas of *la France profonde.* Anyone will tell you about the origin of the name Mormoiron: it comes from the murmur of the bees, their hives were dropped among the invading Saracens so many years ago, and their buzzing saved the village.

The village roofs of Mormoiron are huddled together, making a dull orange sea of ridges, which are occasionally interrupted by the highest branches of some large wisteria bush clinging protectively to the wall. The village has its peculiarities, but they mostly resemble those of other villages. The women who have had children, and those who have not, or cannot, do not get along. The names of those to be conscripted were decided here during the war, with youths arriving from a neighboring town, their trousers splattered with mud from the unpaved roads leading in. Besides its one grocery store, two butchers, and two bakers, it has a fountain at its heart, around which to gossip about times old and new. Up the hill is a baroque-style church, reached by a street with wide stone steps between two rows of houses. There are a few concerts there on summer evenings—and the steps are just right for lingering upon, day or night. So is the street behind, leading up to the *mairie,* where the notary goes when he is not notarizing.

Near the large communal stone basin for washing clothes, there stands in all seasons an old lady in a hat, wearing the same dress, and carrying a small suitcase. She looks out from under her hat always longingly, for she has always loved one man, who first lived with her sister, although he had been "promised" to her. She has waited for fifty years, in all weathers, her packed bag under her arm, for him to pick her up now that her sister is dead. Alas, he now lives with another, and, at 85, "La Jeanne" is still waiting by the communal washing basin, with her bag and her hat.

THE VAUCLUSE

The Vaucluse (the "closed-in valley"—*vallis clausus*) is located in the Comtat Venaissin, home to "the Pope's Jews," who were given refuge here. Our village lies, like so many others with their church and their fountain, near the Mont Ventoux, Thomas Jefferson's mountain, and Petrarch's before him, who climbed up the mountain, reading from his book of St. Augustine's *Confessions,* just as Jefferson read from his Petrarch, in whose steps he was following.

So many tales here, so much tradition. It all clings to the red clay paths you can wander in, the Gallo-Roman tombs of the very folklore-ridden Mazan, to all the chapels on the hilltops, from where the villagers used to signal each other. The oldest synagogue in France is found in Carpentras, the main town of the region. Forbidden to let its ceiling be higher than the stately church of Saint-Siffrein directly in front of it—which has a *porte juive,* a door through which Jewish converts could pass—the architect of the synagogue designed a ceiling with stars upon it, so that symbolically it far overreached the cathedral. It was in the Jewish cemetery of Carpentras that, a few years ago, a recently buried body was dug up and displayed, to the horror of all of France. A prank of children, said the local inhabitants. In any case, François Mitterrand, the president of France, came down from Paris and there was a penitential procession through the streets—oddly echoing a famous procession of the *Penitents blancs*, the penitents dressed in white robes who walked from Mormoiron to Carpentras in the nineteenth century and gave their name to a chapel in the town. When I came the following summer and inquired from my neighbors who could have committed this outrage, the reply was "oh, it must have been the children." Quite like "the Japanese" who took away my olive trees—crimes are always ascribed, as they are everywhere, to "the other."

The villages of the Comtat Venaissin (the region around Venasque, with its 11th century crypt) include the villages of Caromb, Le Barroux, Modène, Saint-Pierre de Vassols, Crillon-le-Brave, Bédoin, Mazan, and Mormoiron. An ancient road leads up past La Gabelle (the town from where the bees were unleashed against the Saracen invaders) and the river La Nesque, whose nearby gorges are staggering in their plunges and swerves, heading toward

Sault, home of the famous lavender fields. On this road, in 1983, Latin inscriptions were discovered, and everywhere there are traces of the former inhabitants—like the Roman wall below my cabanon, or the Roman road leading down from the hilltop. The Knights Templar in the 12th century built their chapels all around here, and many of their remains have been restored. Ah, what lurid tales there are around these chapels: priests burned alive, ex-votos stolen, penitents flagellating themselves in former times, and the present devout; less dramatic, but still arriving in pilgrimages made by foot and now by car, past our cabanon, which usually sees very few passersby.

Why, I wonder as I make my way down to pick up the tall chair I had *"rempaillée"* or restrawed last week, are there so very many cars coming up my hill? I overhear the answer in the village, when I am picking up my oak leaf salad and some *craquante*, and a bunch of bright radishes to serve with butter, French style. Today, an elderly woman is explaining to a bright-eyed younger one, looking very Parisian in style, about the bi-yearly Pilgrimage up to the chapel, which explains that long parade of cars up my hill. And it explains the chapel's bell, ringing at all hours—the tradition being that when you go up the hill the first time, you ring the chapel bell. It is never rung other than that, unless to mark an important occasion.

There are two pilgrimages a year: the 25th of March, to

pray for the ill; and the 2nd of August, to pray for rain: the feasts of the Annunciation and the Transfiguration. I remember many many years ago, when Hilary went up, on foot of course, to pray for rain, under a sky brilliant in Provençal sun . . . and suddenly, there was a downpour. Everyone around always credited her with having wrought some sort of miracle, since we had not seen rain for ages. "*Ah, Hilaire,*" my neighbors teased my tiny red-haired daughter with her pure green-blue eyes and her singular way of understanding animals and people, "*la prochaine fois, toi, tu pries un peu moins, ok?*" Would she pray less the next time, please, so there would only be a light rain, and she just smiled a little. She took things seriously, and animals and people took her seriously also.

Once there was a very celebrated wall: "*le mur de la malédiction*"—the wall of misfortune, or the "mur de la Ligne," intended to isolate the Comtat Venaissin from the plague infested regions. It was, like all the walls in our region, built of dry stone (*pierres sèches*)—without cement—a term that gave its name to René Char's collection *Contre une maison sèche*. The wall stretched from the high village of Murs to Cabrières d'Avignon, on the road to Aix, running through the Fontaine de Vaucluse (Petrarch's haunt).

In nearby Bédoin, at the foot of the Mont Venoux, there was once the ruin of an ancient ice storage and selling facility demolished in July 1974, to clear a path for the *moulin à huile*. It had been called "La Vabane ou Glacière de Fare," and provided a living for the various inhabitants of Bédoin who used to gather the snow from the Ventoux and keep it on planks, under a layer of holly, and when in the summer it turned to ice, they piled it in jars before taking it to other places of storage. The people of nearby villages went to fetch their ice from "Saucisse," one of the carriers.

Among the many traditions of this region is the asparagus feast, and then, on June 24, or *la Saint-Jean*—there is the Feast of Cherries, at the summer solstice, a time of fire and purification. The young girls are supposed to skip bravely over the low blaze of a fire (or its embers) in order to find a husband that year. On August 4, during the pilgrimage to pray for rain—many villagers, and some curious visitors, walk up our hill to the chapel for the ceremony, held partly in *patois* or the local dialect. Then they all consume cakes in the form of a crown (*"les tourtihado"*), before general dancing in the village. On the 15th of August the feast of the Annunciation is held again at Notre-Dame-des-Anges. And, still, the roar of motorbikes occasionally drowns out the memory of pilgrimages: the noise of *la motocrosse* is powerful against everything but memories and traditions. Part of the duty of neighborhoods is to preserve those, however we can.

CHAR COUNTRY

Our family went on repeated visits to see the poet René Char, in Les Busclats, on the Saumane road out of L'Isle-sur-la-Sorgue prior to moving to Provence. We would bring our two children—"each lovelier than the other," he said of them, and a bit later, when we moved there that same summer, after buying our cabanon—the children were for him "like poppies and cornflowers in the wheat fields." And it reminded me of one of his poems about crops and grain that I had translated:

Restore to Them

Restore to them what is no more present in them,

They will see again the harvest grain enclosed in the stalk and swaying on the grass.

Teach them, from the fall to the soaring, the twelve months of their face,

They will cherish their emptiness until their heart's next desire;

For nothing is shipwrecked or delights in ashes;

And for the one who can see the earth's fruitful end,

Failure is of no moment, even if all is lost.

It seems to me now that, at least unconsciously, we wanted to have our children grow up near Char. He would keep two pictures of them in his bookcase, one of Matthew trudging up the hill with a yellow plastic jug of water, in the days we had none, and the other of Hilary in a pine forest, on the top of a neighboring hill, her head to one side, listening to something with the wind blowing through her hair. *Renéchar,* our children would call him, *Renéchar,* sending him notes and drawings, from wherever they were.

Whenever they visited him, he would take them for walks in his back garden, or to pick melons or potatoes. He would buy great bags of marshmallows and jelly candies from the pharmacy for them, placing them by the crates of potatoes and melons, and the books of his poetry he would give me. Char persuaded Charrier, the mayor of Carpentras, to give our children special permission to borrow books from the Bibliothèque Inguebertine to take home and read in their tent. They especially loved the comic books of *Tintin,* like all French children, and devoured book after book.

We were living in René Char's country, and we all loved his village, L'Isle-sur-la-Sorgue, with its massive black mill wheels spinning round in the river, moss dripping with the water from the blades, bright in the sunlight. These waterwheels had marked Char's childhood, and they were to mark that of our children, like a heritage passed on:

Declaring a Name

I was ten. The Sorgue enshrined me. The sun was singing the hours on the water's wise sundial. Sorrow and lack of care had sealed the weathercock on the roofs of the houses and took their support from each other. But what wheel in the child's heart, as he watched, was turning more forcefully, more rapidly, than that of the mill in its white fire?

We'd often go and look at the waterwheels before going to see him in his house in our old sardine can of a car, one of those now-extinct 2 CV (*Deux Chevaux*), with their roll-back canvas tops and their high-fitting chassis, perfect for going across the fields and originally made for the farmers to haul potatoes and crops. Char gave us the stones to build our work table on, saying: "You will build your house on poetry." He was later to give me his "secret of life," a tall bottle filled with a dark liquid of sage, labeled *L'Elixir des Busclats,* an elixir from his house, "*les Busclats.*" "If ever you are depressed, or something goes wrong," he said, "remember you have only to open this. Whatever is wrong will come right," he told me. My faith in Char and in the Elixir was always to remain firm, but I have so far never had to open the bottle.

I would come over in later years during my January vacation from teaching, to work with him on my translations of his poetry. I would spend the night in a small hotel right on the river Sorgue, where the owner, dressed totally in black, once sized me up and said,

"René Char sent you? *C'est un pur.*"

Yes, he was always himself, purely himself, authentic, indeed:"*un pur,*" just like our neighbor Jean-Marie, as small as Char was large. They were both of them "*des purs.*"

In our cabanon, on the hearth in the corner and on all the bookshelves there stand tall earthenware jugs of dried lavender, much of it having come from Char's garden. He would gather it at the end of a long afternoon of working together. Earlier, he would have broiled lamb chops in the fireplace by his desk, under the photograph of Georges Braque, serving them with the lightly fried eggplant his friend Tina Jolas would have prepared as he liked it best, with a *coulis de tomate.* She might have started us off with her *soupede poireaux et pommes de terre/Leek and potato soup,* and ended with melons fresh from the garden, which the children loved to gather when they were visiting their great friend the poet.

Afterwards, Char would have ground the coffee, holding the wooden grinder between his knees and turning the metal handle on top, until the ground beans filled the little drawer at the bottom. He would smile mysteriously at the conclusion of the task, as if there had been something magical about the whole thing.

I treasure each memory from our times with René. It might have been one of those days when he had gone behind his house to pick melons and potatoes with the children, before giving them their *goûter* of chocolate and biscuits, perhaps one of those days when he had to put a bandage on our daughter Hilary's leg, scraped in the briars when she had taken his beloved dog Tigron to walk in the fields. A very good day.

When he came to visit our cabanon, instead of our visiting him, it was because our small Matthew, a particular favorite of his, had fallen off the wall of the upper part onto the lower, cracked his skull badly, and just barely survived. Our neighbor Alain had left his cementing work and dashed Matthew to the hospital. On his return, Char came to see us in the cabanon, to cheer Matthew up, and chose to sit on an upturned grape crate, so as not to split the canvas of our only chairs. He looked about, and his eyes filled with tears:

"*Cela me rappelle du le maquis,*"

he said. "It reminds me of the maquis." And ever after, that crate reminded us of our poet, as did so much else, from the books to the jugs of lavender on the shelves.

There were many things we would all do, and be conscious of, because of Char. I would gather the branches from the sweet-smelling shrubs around our little stone house and make a bath for us all, to help ward off insects, and much more. Char and all our neighbors here believed in *sourciers,* those diviners whose bent twigs the water sources would set trembling: the village superstitions grew to be as precious to us as the traditions and the legends, about which he would give books to the children. Char was, as he knew, protecting us from things that we didn't even suspect might have harmed us. He gave us a talisman of stone to put on our chimney mantel, and cards with his sayings on them to stick on our plaster walls. Here are some of them:

> Obey your pigs, who exist. I obey my gods, who don't.

> Lean over, lean over more. The poet doesn't always leave his page without some mark on him, but like the poor man, he knows how to profit from the eternity of an olive.

Anyone who comes into this world and upsets nothing deserves neither respect nor patience.

If you have to leave, lean against a dry house. Don't worry about the tree, thanks to which, from far off, you will recognize it. Its own fruits will quench its thirst.

That dry house was one of the *bories,* or Ligurian dwellings, that dot the landscape around the old cabanons. There were many superstitions about these dwellings built without mortar, that held for centuries, separately and in clusters. There is, near Gordes—a cliffside village where I would often bike—a whole *village des bories.* "Holding together" like those houses was one of the things Char taught us, without making a big deal of it, and there were, of course, the more practical things we learned from him. Always to bring in your tools from working outside, at twilight. They might rust in the dew. Char taught us how to build, and how to preserve—walls, roofs, and tempers. You keep butter cool in a porous pot hung high in the breeze, and he taught us how you keep poetry living, its stones holding without mortar, like that dry house. He taught by example and image and through stories in the local dialect or patois. Stories about Provençal heroes and monsters and friends. Stories about the Resistance, about his life, about his poetry.

The children would go out at night to look at the constellation he identified himself with: Orion.

Escaped from the Archipelago

Orion,

Pigmented by infinity and earthly thirst,

No longer whetting his arrow on the ancient
    sickle,

His countenance darkened by the calcinated
    iron,

His foot always ready to avoid the fault,

Was content in our midst

And remained.

Whispering among the stars.

It was like learning that criticism, poetry, and their translation into each other might some day meet on common ground. A "*commune présence,*" Char entitled his own selection of his poetry. All the qualities of moral intelligence that his country represented for him at the best of times, that country, now ours, became for us. When, one day, he declared, with a certain solemnity:

"*Vous êtes devenus Pays,*"
You have become Country,

I knew it was of *his* countryside that we had finally become part. We remained so.

THE WINDY MOUNTAIN

Like Char's mountainous figure, our countryside's mountain, the Mont Ventoux, dominated our view of the horizon from the beginning. All the villages in its shadow feel its presence, day and night.

To go up the Mont Ventoux, you can start from Bédoin, seven kilometers from Mormoiron, or from Malaucène, on the other side. From miles around, Mont Ventoux is used as a landmark. Its history, its myth, its legends date from as far back as the history of Provence itself. The Mont Ventoux was the Renaissance poet Petrarch's mountain, the one that brought back Roman times for him and made him value differently the idea of place. La Fontaine de Vaucluse, near L'Isle-sur-la-Sorgue, was the spring he cared about, associating it with his love of Laura. The "closed valley" of the Vaucluse *(Vallis clausus)* stretches between those landmarks, between a spring and a mountain.

A whole tradition penetrates every segment of the road up le Ventoux. It is, and has always been thought of as, a special mountain, uniquely Provençal. Extensive, majestic, and bare of vegetation on top, it rivets the eyes. There are no other mountains nearby, only rolling terraces. It towers above everything. It holds together the different parts of the countryside, just as Char and his poetry gather the separate ways of seeing this part of France, le Midi. You could sometimes judge the temper of the people around here by the color of the mountain, as seen from my bike path. I would surmise the mood of our poet by either the cloudiness of the Ventoux, or its clarity.

That the Mont Ventoux should be also a choice breeding ground for vipers in no way harms its evocative reputation. People are used to making the antidote for viper bites from vipers—the circular logic stirs the imagination. But that great and windy mountain from which the mistral blows, inhabited by a long and precious tradition, has not always been treated as it deserves. When it seemed, a few years ago, about to be besmirched by electronic installations, Picasso, in a fireman's helmet, and René Char, in an Indian headdress, protested violently, to no avail. Some ugly device now sits upon it "like a suppository," as Char put it, irreverently and exactly. Around it, the bare ground is whitish, where the pines cease to grow.

Bare as it is, the Ventoux is held responsible for many events in the region: for the mistral wind, and for the clear sky. For too many visitors and too little work. For the regional wine, flinty and fruity at once, and for visitations of various spirits and for poetic myths. Roman tales are associated with it, as well as those of more recent times. René Char told me a tale of his childhood: he was guarding his grandfather's sheep on the Ventoux, and was afraid of the surrounding wolves. Yet he fell asleep, and the next morning found himself surrounded by a circle traced by a wolf claw, to protect him. The poem he wrote about that occasion, "Marmonnement," which I have translated as "Mumbling," speaks of that fear and that ironic and mystical protection by the trace of a wolf's claws in the earth around him, as he lay sleeping:

MUMBLING

Not to surrender and so to take my bearings, I offend you, but how in love with you I am, wolf, wrongly called funereal, moulded with the secrets of my back country. In a mass of legendary love you leave the trace, virgin, hunted, of your claw. Wolf, I call you, but you have no nameable reality. Moreover, you are unintelligible. By default, compensating, what else could I say? Behind your maneless running, I am bleeding, weeping; I gird myself with terror, I forget. I am laughing under the trees. Pitiless and unending pursuit, where all is set in

motion against the double prey: you invisible
and I perennial

Go on, we endure together; and together,
although separate, we bound over the tremor of
supreme deception to shatter the ice of quick
waters and recognize ourselves there.

The Ventoux is marked, up its impressively winding road,
by the gravestones of those intrepid bikers who made it
only part way up. When I first came, Jean-Marie said to me
with reverence: "the biker Simpson. . . ." Now there is a
plaque to mark where that American biker fell, never to
rise again. His comrades are said to have given him
whiskey to start him on his way once more; the drink was
deadly, in the end mortal. Often you see some group of
bikers gathered there, in his memory. Those legends are
linked forever in my mind: this mountain, and a kind of
courage, foolhardy or not. On the years when the Tour de
France climbs this road, we gather to celebrate the bikers,
our mountain, and its enduring history.

In our first years here, I thought I would find myself
ambling over in our 2CV to the other side of the mountain to Malaucène to learn Provençal and to speak the
patois of the region. As it turns out, the trips I have made
and make now in the language and in the car have a more
modest radius. There is enough language near at hand, and

the rapid-fire Vauclusian French of my neighbors, who occasionally speak in the local *patois,* is enough of a challenge: I don't need to travel.

LIVING HISTORY

In our kitchen, once the stable, from which all those wheelbarrow loads of earth had to be removed, the large rectangular red tiles reach the plastered walls. Some leaves from the ivy and the nearby trees blow in from time to time through the always-opened door. I generally spread a very bright yellow piece of oilcloth over the farm table we purchased in Carpentras, which is sizable enough to seat a good-sized cluster of family or friends in the tiny room, in bad weather when we are unable to sit outside. A bunch of dried flowers, blue and yellow, with a few sprigs of white, has always rested in the round iron cartwheel suspended from a wooden peg on the side wall, the one that tends to become damp with moisture from the deep earth in which it plunges.

Overhead we hung another larger cartwheel to hold the net bags of vegetables: purple eggplant, green squash, white and yellow onions and the purple ones from Simiane. A clump of bay leaves, and the braided strings of garlic heads and clusters of lemons we would have gotten at the Friday market in Carpentras, would often top off the collection. Some of the iron spokes we found in the field by the cherry trees upstairs now protrude from the walls, holding our cooking tongs and forks. All the things we use for daily living have their own past, the biggest being the *tian,* the large pottery vessel traditionally used to hold everything from vegetables for the *ratatouille* to the *fruits confits* from Apt. Many are the wonderful recipes for the *tian,* which gives dishes a special flavor. For us, it also holds our provision of fresh herbs for the day's cooking. Near the tiny stove, a smattering of wooden spoons stands in an earthenware pot.

On the table, we usually have piled up some old, uneven wooden platters and heavy bowls: heaps of crimson tomatoes, green beans, white and pink peaches, and frail golden apricots. Different sizes of potatoes are gathered in the woven baskets, and leaning against the wall we have placed the long three-pronged wooden fork or *fourche* from Buis-les-Baronnies we first got to gather the brambles, as they had to be cut every year. By its side there has always stood our only "*meuble*" or real piece of furniture: a tall cabinet of cherrywood that reaches to the ceiling, with bottles, glasses, and heavy Provençal tablecloths below, and above, three open shelves with rails, where yellow plates rest on their edges behind the piles of matte brown or dull greenish-blue plates and bowls. Holding pride of place is a teapot from our first visit to Aix, painted an old yellow color with tiny red roses on it.

And then, every year we would pick up a little jug or plate from a superb woman potter on the way to Le Barroux, whose colorfully painted signboard first drew us in. The singular style of her high cheekbones and quiet manner seemed to pass over into her pottery.

"Ah!" she says, "you translate René Char! *C'est un pur, n'est-ce pas?*"

This was just what the hotelkeeper at L'Isle-sur-la-Sorgue had said to me when I first arrived one January. Yes, Char was always just that: authentic unto himself, *un pur.*

Le Barroux pottery seems to have a somber sheen to it, glazed in places and matte in others—the pieces feel at once rough and smooth to the touch, and what is served in them seems to taste different from what is placed on the light-brown earthenware *grès* plates I bought upon first arriving. The *grès* is heavy, heavy, and when you cut on it, it makes a satisfying noise. The handmade bowls of light greenish-blue and deep purplish-black actually shimmer in the light: I put tomatoes or cucumbers in them, and in the smaller ones, slices of lemon to set off the darkness of the color, like the Spanish still lifes of Cotán, with the vegetables piled up against the black background. Often the kitchen table feels like a gathering of Spanish still life.

Outside against the downstairs wall, crumbling in places, is an iron boot-scraper, on which we would always sun our melons, like round orange beacons, for our way up the steep stone steps to the upper room. Upstairs, in the tiny room where the owner used to nap, you see just a bed, a little wooden table, a wooden *armoire* in the corner, and a trunk covered with the same Provençal material as the bed, at once luminous and dark, deep gold and black in a pattern of paisley and stripe. As for the great beams holding up the roof, an extra one has been placed on either side of the one in the center, because the latter is almost entirely scooped out by carpenter ants, in spite of my admittedly irregular attention to it with Xylophène, the anti-ant product you squirt through into all the little holes left by them, hoping eventually to see fewer little piles of wood droppings on the floor or the books below.

There is a small yellow wooden door that marks a cabinet with shelves deep in the thick stone wall. A few leaves gather on the floor when the mistral sweeps through the heavy door with its massive medieval-looking lock. In the niche of the *fenestron,* or little slot of a window now closed in, there is a little pile of books for reading in bed: Proust, Hopkins, Henry James, Jane Austen, Baudelaire, Swinburne, Woolf. Outside, against the wall, is a rough stone basin from which the horse used to drink. Over it hangs a grapevine. The grapes ripen at the end of the summer, growing more purple by the day. A large table is placed in the field here, among the grasses and the wild flowers, where you can sit looking at cherry trees at the end of the field, observe the way the light changes, from the sunshine of early morning to the late darkness lit only by stars. The ground of the field is uneven, where daisies grow in their season, and, early in the summer, poppies, as well as some bluish grass. You can still see a few sparse vines from a former vineyard poking up through the assorted flowers. From the field, you can just see the red roof of our friends Malcolm and Janet up the hill. They have been there since my family and I have been here. We arrived together.

Upon the white plaster walls that we had to patch on occasion, there are taped bouquets of dried flowers we or our friends have gathered, and posters of ancient stone heads from Cluny, of Maurice Denis and the Nabis, and various museum exhibitions. Behind the bed, in a large reproduction of a Pisanello painting I brought back from Verona, a horse turns its head away and displays its hindquarters, and young faces look out with what I imagine to be affection. On the side wall there has always hung a series of straw hats, for us and our visitors to protect against the unpardoning sun. Logs used to burn in the fireplace in the winter, and we would toast marshmallows on some of the old iron cooking tools hanging on both sides, along with the handheld pokers and long forks. Alas, because of the dormice who loved to come in and join us, or then nibble the mattresses, we eventually had to cement it up. As for the rust-colored stains above the mantel, I was told that if you rub them with 27 cloves of garlic, they will disappear, but we never tried it.

Along the road, beyond another hedge of rosemary bushes upon yet another dry wall, at all hours of the day and night a few cars pass by, and a motorbike or two, and then the occasional walkers, ready for the climb uphill to Notre-Dame-des-Anges itself. We walk up there sometimes also, to the top where the blue Virgin stands above the chapel. After the vineyards beside the chapel, a very narrow Roman road leads the way down, its highly irregular stones worn and with their faint inscriptions covered over. This path leads down through the underbrush to return to our cabanon, which seems even now always in need of being restored. It feels like a place of peace, among the oak trees, the remaining few olive trees, the cherry trees, and the almond trees, with their green bittersweet nuts, a few tall bushes with small black berries, several rosemary shrubs along the walls, a few clumps of thyme alongside them, and then some sage. At sunset we walk, with whatever visitors we might happen to have, down to look at the sunset, out over our village.

THE OLIVE TREES

Olive trees, wherever they are, have always meant Provence to me. They glitter in the sun and stand tall. Not as tall as the oaks, of course, nor tall as the cherry trees that form the border of our land. They are vastly more important, though. They stand watch, I like to think, over our cabanon, our little stone house surrounded by so much foliage. You can't see it from the street, and, unless you knew, you would always be surprised it was there at all. The haphazard branches and growth shield the cabanon from any outside world, it seems.

Of course, our land is overgrown, and the brambles always push back up as proud as can be. Everyone knows that brambles overrun everything if left to themselves, that they grow long and menacing in the open, and hide in unsuspected places as well. They can foil the meanest tools and the most long-suffering gardener, yet I really used to believe that there was a way we might win out. It wasn't that I meant to clean out the entire garden below and field above it, or liberate every single tree and bush from the vines and brambles. No, I just thought I might clear the way from the kitchen to the back wall, where a cousin had built a stone chair for the children and me right into the wall, to sit on, away from everyone. So we would have our very own space, like the olive trees outside. The chair, alas very difficult to get to through the brambles, has arms wide enough to put one's cold drink on, or so I remember it at least. I can't reach it as often as I would like, for the brambles frequently win out.

In the beginning I thought perhaps with two hours a day, I could eventually free us from the menace of the brambles. So I would put on my straw hat and my thick green rubber gloves, once in the early morning and again in the late afternoon, when the sun had gone aslant, and set off with my circular tree saw. I was to develop over the course of the summer a certain technique for dealing with them, cutting them as near to the ground as possible, but never trying to pull the whole thing out at once, as the branches will have grown in their own ways and will not yield in two directions at once. So I would make two or three cuts up the long stem, pulling from the bottom and cutting at the top anything that would not give. Of course, I discovered that brambles are wilier even than you think. They seem to attach themselves at both ends; you cut one end, and the other is simply awaiting its time to spring back. Never mind, I did what I could each day. When I had enough brambles to make a load, I would gather them up with the long *fourche* or wooden field fork, and lift them high over my head to toss them down in the next lot—the one we had never been allowed to buy.

I know how useless all this must have seemed, because the brambles would grow right back the next year. But it felt like a sort of moral duty, until there came a point one summer when I realized that there are, indeed, some things in nature that you absolutely can't win against, with all the stubbornness in the world and in you. As for the little stone chair in the wall, we all know it's still there, and I expect we'll get to it some day.

But there were always those olive trees that had to be "liberated," as I thought of it. And I refused to give up. Now, I know terms like that may not be the right categories for plants and trees, as if I were to have mixed them up with humans. I suspect René Char's teachings have something to do with all my thinking here.... In any case, the way I have always seen life here had started years before, when we first came to the cabanon. I had always gotten up at five in the morning to remove all the growth around and in the olive trees, because the poet I had loved and trusted had come here to the cabanon, and told me how the olive was jealous of anything in its way. It needed its space to grow in and be content. Of course, a content olive tree produces the happiest olives, for the happiest nourishment. In any case, for Char, animals and plants needed the same care as people, yet another thing he taught us, in a kind of learning epiphany about the distinct philosophy of life here in Provence.

Even at those times when you realize the brambles have you beaten, you can see how the ivy grows thick up the walls, how the light falls differently in the different months on the large field up to the spring. You can listen to the sounds of the birds and crickets, and the different sounds of your friends, when you have them over to sit under your trees, or you go to sit under theirs. So, really, the brambles and overgrowth are as much a part of this place as the light, the melons, the olive trees, the animals, and our friends.

THE ANIMAL KINGDOM

Overhead in the upper room, in the night and even the early evening, as they grew more used to family living, the dormice began to disport themselves upon the old beams high above the bed. For these engaging animals the size of squirrels, or *loirs,* with long tails and bright eyes, and endowed with a delightful squeaky enunciation, the *patois* name was something that sounded like *grigouirra.* Jean-Marie could not spell it, he said, but it sounded just like they look. So cozy and cute that you might not even begrudge them their appetite for mattresses and pillows.

For here, in reference to these little creatures and other aspects of rural life, the split between *patois* as it is spoken by my neighbors, as they work in the cherry trees and vines, and the French we learn in school or in Paris is very clear. Here, taking off the little branches with buds— *"débourgeonner"*—becomes what sounds like *"démaillenquer,"* and the instrument you work with, which we would call *"la pioche,"* is an *"ixade"*—while pulling out the grass at the foot of the vines is to *"faire délailles"*—I will never learn, but will always admire this working language. It is like the "*grigouirra,*" a sound itself crammed full of meaning.

To the children, in place of their bedtime story, when our imaginations and the Narnia tales were exhausted, I would read pages of Elizabeth David's descriptions of markets and melons. In their tent outside, they envied our bedding beneath the squeaking and scurrying of the dormice, endlessly curious and good-tempered, with their bright eyes sparkling. Rather like our children themselves. The *grigouirra* seemed to be interested in people's working and sleeping, in everything that went on in that room, not just in the pillows and mattresses they could devour when we left for the New York winter.

However, given their squeaking and their gustatory habits, they brought certain drawbacks for our would-be-calm lives. So we finally resorted to the "Have-a-Heart Trap" we had brought over with us for just such a purpose. This contraption in no way harmed the animals caught in it, which had to be smallish, of necessity, and from which they could simply emerge when the door was opened. When a *loir* crawled in, we would make a family expedition to the top of the hill, tell it a briefer bedtime story, wish it well, and let it go. Sometimes, if she was in the mood, Hilary would play it a tiny tune on her recorder, as she did in New York when we let her hamsters go in various parts of Central Park. We were, of course, not surprised at the frequent returns of the dormice, perhaps the ones we had liberated, perhaps others, for they liked family living as much as we did, and had adopted us.

As opposed to our hillside in Mormoiron, it's so cold on the Ventoux, where we would liberate the mice, that I always take extra coats along for everyone in the car, which we all wrap ourselves in, dizzied by the height of our own great mountain and the intense cold. We take hikes, we get blown along to the stone orientation construction atop the lookout point. We'd sometimes pick some large mushrooms, but always making sure to take a sample to the pharmacist, to be sure they were not poisonous. Later, we'd put them in an omelet with garlic and oil, sprinkled with chives or *ciboulette,* and have a post-mountain feast, along with the *ratatouille* made earlier, no need to reheat it. .

Picnics often lead to music, and the children would belt out a song they learned in school:

> *Il Il y avait un taureau–o–o*
> *Qui vivait à Mexico–o–o*
> There was once a bull
> Who lived in Mexico—

I don't know where it went from there.

Me, I recalled from my days with outings from Paris with my French groups, songs like

> *Colchiques dans les prés*
> *fleurissent fleurissent*
> *colchiques dans les prés*
> *fleurissent au mois de mai*

> Poppies in the fields
> flowering flowering
> poppies in the field
> flower in the month of May

I could see them now, all red poppies, spreading out as far as the eyes could see. I remember our car trips, all singing at the top of our lungs: RULE BRITANNIA / BRITTANIA RULE THE WAVES.

ALMONDS AND CHERRIES

In one particular memory, set early in the morning before the great heat descends like a hammer, I see a field of tall grass, studded with a few red poppies bending in the wind, clumps of yellow *pissenlits* or dandelions in happy chaos, and some lavender flowers stretching out above the rest toward the cherry trees. They and the *oliveraie*, the great circle of olive trees I used to love so much, before the central root was taken, were the first thing I remember about our cabanon Biska. They had their own way of being, and were a good part of our being as well.

Those olive trees used to shine in the lower garden, marking the way to the stone seat made in the wall for me to hide in, behind the brambles, away from the sun or from the visitors. Above, in the upper terrain, are ranged the cherry trees that can live about a hundred years. When we arrived, the long row that led from the cabanon door still belonged to the former owner of the cabanon, who would come to pick the cherries. Even when my neighbor Serge picked, with his family, all the cherries of the trees in the far field, the cherry tree by the bedroom door remained our own. Now I go out to gather a few cherries the first thing in the morning, or after breakfast, or mid-morning, or any time, during the weeks in May and June when they hang heavy on the trees.

I remember those first years, when, with the children, I used to climb up in those trees in all weathers, tossing the cherries down into the great woven baskets on the ground or taking a basket up with me, the round kind with a high handle to suspend from the branches. You cannot sell cherries without the stems, and it is said to be better for the tree to remove them along with the cherries.

My cherry trees are now middle-aged, the ones that

remain, although new ones seem to be strangely springing up. They give their fruit in late May and early June, before we come to Provence, and before the ones in the far end of the field. Those far ones are *Coeur-de-Pigeon,* which the people from here call the pointed ones, "*les pointus,*" because they are narrow at one end. If they sell at a good price, it makes it worthwhile for the neighbors to pick them and take the profit; otherwise, whoever has the time goes for an hour or two in the morning before the heavy heat or in the evening. Down the hill are Alain's cherries he has invited us to pick: the *Smiths* (pronounced Les Smits) and the *Belges,* larger, he says. I can't actually taste them as well as the *Burlats,* so rich in flavor. Nor can I taste the big white *napoléons,* of which many are so fond, and which are also part of Alain's cherries. We haven't had time or energy to go that far yet. It takes energy, living in a cabanon, making your way up the steps, moving chairs from one place to another, avoiding the cracks in the wall and the holes here and there, dealing with the age-old locks and massive doors. And the rest.

My cherries glisten in the rain and the sun; they are sweet and dark, the *Burlats* near the house, the *Coeur-Pigeon* or *les pointus* farther off, redder and smaller, and the *napoléons* farther on, in the orchard. Their profusion against the brilliant sky is enough to make you believe in something. So is the way they gleam in the rain.

In the evening, after supper, I set the ones I have gathered out on the table in great bowls, letting them spill over a little on the cloth. Their short-livedness is part of their magic; oh, I have tried to preserve them, in little and larger jars, to make jam and *cerises à l'eau-de-vie,* and am gradually using up the latter I have previously stored. The *eau-de-vie* means you do not have to go through the tedious paraffin-sealing procedure: you can let the fruit sit outside to ferment for up to three months before sealing the lids— in any case, nothing can go wrong. From time to time I tell myself that it is useless to try to keep them, to try to hang on to their sweetness. That it takes too much time away from just living amidst them, when they are there. I should conserve my own energy for what is here and now, rather than the fleeting beauty of the cherries.

STAIRS AND PASSAGES

Down the stone stairs that are too high to be reassuring, you can see the downstairs table for work and meals and tea. It is also the table for sitting around with a *pastis* or a syrup, and it is the center of our evenings if we're not too many, in which case we dine upstairs in the field. The table is really an old door, rescued from a house torn down, that rests upon flat white-yellow stones in a sort of natural arch of trees bending over, their leaves interweaved. Beyond this, I have laid a square of old stones, fitting the straight sides together into the ground. In the morning, the table is covered with a bright cloth of blue olives and yellow flowers, or one of dull yellow with tiny dark red flowers. In the evening, I prefer a cloth of lavender color with sprigs of lavender printed on it. I set a jug of Char's dried lavender in the middle, and their scent gives me a feeling of calm.

At lunch time, on the table outside in the field upstairs, upon the chairs with the woven straw seats, I set down the large straw hats that usually hang on my wall, if I think those coming to lunch will need them against the sun. Merciless, it beams even through the slats of the bamboo cover overhead, called a *canisse*. The slats are held together by thin wires resting on a structure of logs and slender treetrunks; a honeysuckle vine is making its way up, and I try to overlook the fact that its sweet odor often attracts my deadly enemy later on in the summer, the mighty wasp, to which I am more than mightily allergic. After a sting, I have to be rushed to the hospital in Carpentras, which has happened a few times. Once I spent all night there, in a room with another patient who spoke constantly of a wish for suicide, and in the morning our house guest, my colleague Gerhard, was waiting outside to take me home. Never did a journey feel so reassuring as that return.

Sun shines on the ivy, on the side of the house, and on the Roman wall by the table. Telling us, over a *pastis,* how he was once tempted to dig down to his Roman wall, Jean-Marie, a cigarette in the corner of his mouth, said:

> "Ah, yes, I'd have liked to see my wall. But then
> I realized the cherry tree needed water—the
> living have to come before the dead."

The digging might disturb the water source. So he covered the Roman times back up. But everywhere, we have the feeling, and the knowledge, of Roman walls holding us up with their tradition.

Before we had water of our own, Hilary and Matthew would go up the hill with great jugs to get the water from our spring for drinking, washing, living; this was formerly the water for the goats, and each neighbor had a partial right to it. All the *"droits de passage"* or "passage rights," usually to a water source, are oddly complicated. What ground you walk over, which vines you try not to trample, which paths you avoid or take, all of it matters. In earlier times, before there was water from the town, the important thing about this had to do with arriving at the correct time to draw one's water, with or without one's animals, dependent on the source. So one would have the rights on Thursday 3-5, and one on Tuesday 1-3, and the vines would have their hours also. Down by the *bassin* where we got our water when the spring was running, the water used to be rationed out to the neighbors, and the stories were legion, as many and as colorful as in the films *Jean de Florette* and *Manon des Sources*. The water would flow from the spring into a squarish container, whose lid fit heavily upon the contents, the water as precious as gold. At nightfall, it was not a difficult endeavor to shuffle out in your espadrilles and take a bit of water for your own earth and goats, said Tata, because it was far less populated than now.

Years ago, Jean-Marie's father would walk up every day, by the cabanon, to the spring of the Cabanon Biska, convinced it would cure his sniffles if he simply anointed his nose with it. Its magic properties were less visible to me than its fickle behavior. When the ground would shift, and the spring had not come to the surface, or when the spring would dry up in the summer, the problems were dramatic. I would have to go down the hill on my bike to get water from La Brèche, the spigot of always-flowing water on a side street in the village two kilometers away, and bring it back up in a jug, balanced precariously in my market basket on the back of my bike. When René Char came to visit, he had told us how to speak to the spring. We were to say:

"Source, mon amie, coule pour nous."

"Spring, friend spring," we would say, "run gently for us."

Hilary and Matthew went up to speak to the spring, exactly as he had said. He must have meant for us to speak in the Provençal language, as he could, or else it would surely have worked, as it always did when he came. One day we rammed a Sears-Roebuck coil into the pipe, and some water dribbled out. So much for poetry and pragmatics. We captured the dribble of water in a long plastic tube, like a hose, to wash in. It was hot, and not very appealing, so we would continue to go down to La Brèche in the village for our drinking supply. In any case, when the earth moved once more, our own spring was lost underground for good.

At first, we felt alone here, surrounded by strangers, in a land strange to us. That they later became our friends was a wonderful happening whose occurrence we never questioned. The poet had told us that we were *Pays*, part of this country along with him, and so we were bound to be at home here, as much as the olive trees.

PAST TIMES

There is something about time and Provence that I always think I have learned, and time and time again have realized that I have not. Not yet, at least. In Provence, I usually consider that a book comes second to whatever is going on outside—exactly the opposite from my point of view about New York City. I am generally able to put a book down, any book, and emerge into the dawn or even the late morning sun, and get on with living. Or in the evening, to water the vines I am trying to train up the side of the wall, as well as the nearby mulberry trees.

But not in all cases. Take this morning, for example. I am in the middle of re-reading *The Wings of the Dove* and cannot possibly rouse myself before finishing. My children have breakfast, have lunch, peer in at me from time to time to see how it is getting along—but they understand completely. What a singular luxury: reading Henry James in the upper room of a cabanon when, outside, the world is sparkling and you know you are missing it, and yet continue, inside the thick walls, an obsessive plunge into a story you know the ending of. I feel loved, protected in my obsession, understood, not just by my children but by all around me. Time moves differently here, and understanding too.

It moved differently just the other week, at a house in town, where my friends Michel and Mireille live, right behind the post office. They own the tomatoes and vines just across from my cabanon: Michel, with a warm smile, waves from his tractor every day, and Mireille shows me what to plant in my herb patch (which I can scarcely dignify, no matter what I put there, by the name of garden). She has a garden; I have a patch, but am very happy to have it and browse through the thyme, sage, and tarragon, all in uneven quantities, all very small. Only my rosemary bushes and my wild mint could be thought of as plentiful.

Mireille will stop me if we meet at the *boulangerie,* and suggest I come for a drink—she may have the juniper drink she has made from a wild plant growing near a mountain, and serves cool, in a smallish amount. It is bitter and sweet too. Mireille never fails to make her lunch for two into lunch for three, and I never refuse. I always take some of what I have in the car or have just bought at the market. This time, it's some fennel and carrots and cucumber strips I had gotten to serve with my *anchoiade,* and those extraordinary winkles my fishmonger's mother prepares fresh every morning with garlic and parsley. Consuming those puts us all in a remarkably good mood, just like last week, when Mireille made her favorite fish recipes for me, and we sat drinking her orange wine for hours before we had them. She showed me how you shake everything all together for the sauce, and I wrote it down so I wouldn't forget. I have put her recipes in the recipe section.

Today Mireille is positively beaming. Michel grins upon seeing me.

"Ah! Marianne!"

It was Mireille who helped me learn to drive again after my divorce, when the traffic in Carpentras changed to a one-way system. Mireille who taught me how to make sweet herb liquors, and how to put up jam. We exchange gossip, and I am on the point of leaving, when they invite me for pizza on Sunday, around lunchtime:

> "Come at eleven-thirty, if you like," says
> Mireille, "and bring a sweater. It may get cold."

It may get cold? I don't see how it could possibly get cold in this climate at that hour and at this time of year, but I put one in the 2CV just for good luck for when I arrive. But by one-thirty I hadn't yet gotten there. When I did, I saw gathered around the melons, at two long tables spread with white paper, Mireille's entire family: brothers, wives, mothers, children, dogs, and then, me.

Now, my French always fails me at times like these. My accent goes wrong, my vocabulary stops short, my brain sizzles to an absolute halt. I want to participate fully and end up sounding paltry. Anyway, the pizzas begin after the platters and platters of melons ended. Putting on her tall chef's hat and apron, Mireille prepares mixture after mixture: tomato, anchovy, sausage, ham, shrimp, squid, crab; and Michel toasts them on an immensely long stick in the clay pizza oven he built himself. Just the briefest minute or two later, because the oven is so very hot, the pizzas emerge crisp and thin, with an incomparable aroma.

Chilled rosé wine accompanies hundreds of jokes, the tenor of which I get, and the point, but whose general spirit I can't quite enter into: they are at once good-hearted and on the far side of what the French call *grivois*—or then *salées*—spicy, salty, and not what I was supposed to hear in the old South. However, the occasion seems to demand that I respond some other way than with a fixed smile and small laugh. After three or four hours, during which each of the "best" is repeated to assure my having understood, I hope it is time to go home.

How wrong I am. It is now time, although the rain has begun, to play *boules,* and this group is made up of champions. Michel had been stuck with me once in the village tournament, when I hadn't known the rudiments of the game, even the difference between a "*pointe*" and a "*tire.*" You *pointe* when you try to hit the little ball in the center, and you *tire* when you want to knock someone else's ball away from that little center one, the "*bouchon,*" or the *cochonnet.* In any case, I was neither any good at it, nor destined to be any good. Michel's main concern, which he generously did not voice, but which was quite loudly enunciated by the lookers-on, was that we not be the very worst, because then we would be have to "*baiser la Sainte Fanny,*" translated in the *Vocabulaire des boules Lyonnaises* as "*embrasser Fanny.*" I didn't even understand what that meant, on top of the complications of boules.

This is the explanation Mireille gives me: the expression *"baiser la Sainte Fanny"* comes from Marius in Pagnol's play, who arrives too late to marry his Fanny, and she has gone and married another. (In fact, or rather, in this well-believed fiction, Marius, whom she loves, has gone off to sea, torn between love of water and woman. Expecting his child, and not expecting Marius, she has married an older, loving man; Marius returns too late, thus being the loser.) For Michel and myself to end up "kissing Sainte Fanny" on the statue's bare bottom would have been most definitely my fault, and a grave one indeed.

I was to learn other expressions with regards to the game of Boules: to *faire têter,* or to unite oneself so closely with the *bouchon* as to be as suckling and breast, but put in the milder Lyonnais style, it was to be a *biberon,* or bottle. Clearly, the vocabulary of the Midi was more heated, more colorful than that of Lyon. But now in gloomy spirits, because of the loss, I have no desire to repeat the effort. I reiterate with many forceful gestures that it is definitely time for me to go home. It is now six-thirty, and that seems about right for an afternoon: one-thirty to six-thirty. I start the obligatory rounds to kiss everyone goodbye, three times, left, right, left. . . .

"What? Before supper?" asks Mireille, with her warm smile and an expression of disbelief. I mutter something convincing about having to write something or other that I have to then send off. Right now.

"Well, then just come back when you are through, okay?"

It is nice to be wanted, and so I return after a while, after scribbling something at the outside table of the cabanon. There is now red wine being served, hot *merguez* sausage, warm potato salad, and *gâteau de riz,* coconut flavored. Things warm up again. At eleven, I weave my way unevenly back to my 2CV in the drizzle, happy, one headlight up and one down. It seems just the right way to spend an evening.

PAINTING AND POETRY

Just when I get back to the cabanon, my friend the painter Sooky Maniquant phones. Hilary was always surprised that the cabanon could actually accommodate a telephone, since in the beginning, we had—along with no running water, of course no flush toilets, and no light—no modern conveniences. My nostalgia kicks in at that memory, but since having the phone installed (good idea, given my allergy to wasps and such), I am very glad to be in contact with friends and some variety of the world. Sooky was a friend of Char, as so many of us were, and that makes, now, a real community all over France.

"When can you come over to La Claparède?"

Sooky has just finished a superb book of watercolors on Char's poems, to which I wrote the preface. Upon Char's death, she turned from horizon-oriented landscapes to abstract painting. Since she had done the landscapes in relation to his poetry, perhaps it felt too painful to continue them. But she shows us how, in these recent works, you can trace the marks of her brush.

I go the next day, brave and foolhardy, by myself in the 2CV, as if I were not afraid of falling asleep at the wheel—as of course I am—to Sooky's house in Bonnieux. It is at least four hundred and fifty years old, its ancient oak beams dividing the rooms with their deep-set windows. The stones of the house are immense, yet somehow she rebuilt the walls herself. She serves us just-grilled lamb chops *aux herbes de Provence,* a salad of dandelion leaves, a platter of *fromages de chèvre,* and a meringue concoction, followed by a glass of *fine* with the coffee.

Afterward, she shows us the nearby *borie,* one of those "dry houses" from ancient times she has been living in. René Char wrote a long series of aphoristic texts about them, set up as a dialogue with its walls and a speaker, beginning like this:

Against a Dry House

If you must leave, lean against a dry house. Don't worry about the tree by which you'll know it from a distance. Its own fruits will quench its thirst.

Raised before its meaning, a word wakes us, bestows on us the day's brightness, a word that has not dreamed.

Apple-colored space. Space, burning fruit-bowl.

Today is a wild beast. Tomorrow will see it leap.

These round dwellings of flat stones placed, without mortar, simply upon each other, building up and narrowing to the top center, are surviving miracles of the Ligurian age. You build a fire, and the smoke escapes; the rain pours down, and you are dry. You enter by a narrow opening, feeling you are entering one of the smaller pyramids in Egypt, crouching for an uncomfortably long time because of the thickness of the walls. Suddenly you can stand upright, breathe unimpeded, in a recreated space all about you. When I first entered a *borie,* twenty-five years ago in Gordes, I felt I had entered history. Now I know history can be lived in. And it is my painter friend Sooky who has reminded me of this.

At Sooky's table, I meet Robert, a somber-faced painter with finely chiseled features and piercing eyes from nearby Cavaillon, who has always lived in this region. Unsmiling at first, he speaks very slowly to be sure I will understand.

Then, as we speak of French poetry, of Mallarmé and Rimbaud, of Apollinaire and Reverdy, and, of course, of Char, he distinctly warms up. By the end of the day he has invited me to a *Fête des Vins* tomorrow in a little town at the foot of the Ventoux, near Bédoin. Afterwards, he says, we will dine with more painters in a convent chapel.

> *"Toi, tu vis près de nous?"*
> "Do you live near us?"

asks a child of one of the other painters when we are ensconced around a makeshift table in the chapel, feeling like something out of a Last Supper.

> *"Oui,"* I answer, *"tout près."*
> I live very near you.

And think to myself, I always will, if I can. I give the same answer to the young couple in Mormoiron who question me about my returning to Provence, to the Vaucluse. If I can.

Driving down late at night from the chapel, I run straight into a street festival in Bédoin: dodgems, cars spinning about, cotton candy, shooting stands, the smell of caramel apples, pungent sausage smoke rising from the large iron pots. People throng the streets, breaking into smiles at the sight of my old sardine tin of a car ambling along at its favorite pace, about 20 miles an hour. I am in no rush. None of us have been in a hurry these last few days, as I have lived them. I make up my mind to avoid whatever mad rushes I can, even when I return in the winters to New York. I resolve to put a certain slowness into my writing and my living, as things seem to have a better chance of lasting here, where things move slowly.

EXPEDITIIONS AND BELONGING

After all these years here in the cabanon, nothing feels as if it has changed much, in me or without. I still walk up the hill in the early morning, or later, to look back at the village and my small house. Or I might stroll down the hill halfway, to the place, marked by blackberry bushes, where I can cut across and look at the mountain. I pick my walking stick back up and go down the hill toward my empty stone house, in its field amid the trees with cherries and almonds. And melons. I walk down slowly, and if it is late enough in the season, after the cherries of May and June have given way to the blackberries of August, I will reach across the ditch to pick the largest fruits shining dark in the sun. I often pick a few flowers of blue and yellow to put on the bright blue tablecloth, or, later, to stick with tape on the plaster wall.

When I return, having left some Bach recording

resounding, I am always glad to climb over a little stone slab with a bigger one on a different slant beside it, to make my way up the overgrown path to the shaded shelters of bamboo slats stretched over the tree trunks with a lantern hanging under each. There, I take the steep stairs by the basil plants, leading to the other room above, out of whose small windows, framed by a thick mat of ivy on each side, I gaze from time to time. Seen from here, things take on a different perspective, and find a focus they might not have had before.

Four melons stand in a row against the ochre wall which used to have a mass of ivy climbing up, that I try hard not to miss. Apricots in a green glazed bowl rest on the yellow oilcloth, next to the single lemon and the avocado on the green plate. A pile of deep red tomatoes sinks down into the orangish-gray earthenware dish. On the stone steps are two pairs of espadrilles, one of washed-out lavender and the other of palest blue, and two basil plants.

Later in the evening, I am invited by Ann and Clive for a drink on their terrace in Villes, overlooking the orange roofs of a nearby village, a view only interrupted by the steeple of the little church. We sit over our black and green olives, our *tapenade* and *pâté,* as the sun goes down and the stars come out, so bright here. Things seem so simple from this terrace: how to bring this simplicity into my own life?

I belong here. In the land of simple pleasures, inhabited

by "*les purs.*" Belonging here will never be less important to me. I keep the accent of Provence: I say *demaing* and *paing* and feel it is right, here. It is now my language too. It is what I will keep working at and let my desk, and whatever is on it, go. This life feels real.

Besides my solo expeditions into the hillside around my cabanon, there is another sort of expedition that is close to my heart, the kind we would go on with our children. In my family, we have always been very fond of what we think of as genuine expeditions, less tame and more exploratory than the ones we so often made to some of the caves nearby, or then the quarries and woods ten minutes away. Especially when they are accompanied by picnics, the height of gustatory delight for the children and for me too.

We would always set out in our yellow 2CV, in the times when we still called our cabanon by its name, "*Biska.*" We would strap the canvas roof back, quite like a sardine can opened halfway, on our easier expeditions, say, to a high patch of lavender the children called "the end of the world."

We had rules for riding in our beloved car. If we were in a village, the children could "*faire le petit debout,*" standing up halfway, or kneeling on the back seat, and "*le grand debout*" if we were in the countryside, standing full-height so the wind could whistle through their blond hair. I would look in the rear-view mirror to watch them. When others complained about the mistral wind, we found ourselves exchanging smiles. We actually all loved the mistral.

As I remember it now, three more remote places particularly served our imaginations, legs, and tummies. The first was called La Vallée de Picarel. Characterized by high red cliffs, a forest, and a combination of both, it had a path where you could walk for a very long time under the trees arching overhead, ending in a deepish cave, whose walls were of an unforgettable red ochre. Like the famed red cliffs of Roussillon, we thought, but close to us, and not domesticated. Not prettied up, just right for picnics.

We would each find a spot in a niche or on a stone, and take from the picnic basket—whose components were now placed on a folding cane mat in the center of the floor—the parts we best liked for our own plates, and light a candle in the center of the cave, upon the mat. I would stick some dried flowers in a wine bottle, open another bottle, and we would sit, munch, and tell stories. We might have some ham and *pommes de terre aux herbes* served cold, perhaps some melon and fruit, and, if I had remembered to make some, a lentil salad with vinaigrette, pink onions, and lots of basil. We would be supplied with iced tea, or unsweetened lemonade I had just made that morning, and consume our portion like the good cave people we were. Hilary would sometimes play her recorder, very quietly, a rather sad tune, and Matthew might beat time—or not. He sometimes brought his guitar along so they could play together.

We had other cave picnics, along the Gorges de la Nesque, in a high bright spot with the wind raging outside, and, once, the rain . . . these occasions all participated in a celebration of shelter, against the elements, within a past that was not just ours, but that we were continuing from so many others. We would all walk up and occupy separate peaks of the rocks, sit for a while—this was usually in the late evening—and then join forces halfway down by the oak tree to have our picnic.

Or we would go up to the Dentelles de Montmirail, climbing way up the well-worn path, grasping the slight trees and shrubs so as to not slip backward. We might just take a few slices of sausage or a hunk of aged Cantal, accompanied by slices of country bread *(pain de campagne)* with fresh unsalted butter, and tarragon mustard. There would most likely be some *tapenade,* the green kind especially good on picnics. (I will shamelessly take any opportunity to take *tapenade* anywhere at all, just in case an urge comes over me.) I like to take along some oranges drenched in red wine, with a bit of cinnamon or orange peel mixed in: very fortifying after a long uphill walk.

If I went alone, or with just one friend, we would go first thing in the morning, perhaps at seven, before the sun made it untenable, walking in our espadrilles up the slope to the ragged rocks, called the Dentelles or lace, just for that reason. Here I read Eudora Welty, and a great deal of Faulkner—the books are forever marked for me with the sight of those rocks. And the memory, now, of Char's having wanted me to go up farther to consult La Pythie, the mythic sorceress, who could tell your fortune and tales suited to you alone.

Once down, with the children, we would stop at the round tables under the plane trees of the hotel/restaurant Les Florets, on its lovely terrace overlooking the Dentelles. We would have coffee or a drink, or, occasionally a meal. I had lived here for a few days when the cabanon was being divested of hornets and rats, and I translated my first poems of Char, believing as I did in La Pythie, since he had sent me to this place.

In times of depression, I would betake myself alone to these small mountains or large rocks, to meditate on poetry, life, coincidence, and the like. I'd love to say I would return chastened by the bigness of nature, but in fact I would return worn out by my climb and the bumpy drive, undepressed.

GETTING SOME WINE AND MY GOAT

In the early morning, before the great rising of heat, I go to the *cave coopérative* with my five-liter container (my "*cubic*") and some empty bottles. You have a choice of a range of inexepensive wines in their barrels: the winemaker's rosé or blanc or then a special *Carte noire* or some other such bottle made with Syrah grapes, at reasonable prices, for the container; the bottles are filled in the back room, out of sight, with modest table wine. On the display shelves are all qualities of the local variety. I pick up several bottles of white, a few bottles of rosé and two of the special wines Alain gave me last week: one is aged in some particular wood for some particular time, and the other is the heavy Syrah. I roll all of this out on a cart, off of which crashes the rosé to my consternation, making a mess and a waste. The more enthusiastic I get, the more awkward.

I clean it up, return the cart, and make my way to the *boulangerie* to be sure of getting one of the irregularly shaped and long-keeping loaves, the *pain artisanal*, before they are all spoken for. Just enough are made each day, 8 to 10, for the early enthusiasts, among which I certainly number myself. If you get there at, say, ten-fifteen, no luck. Sometimes I like the *pain-épi* shaped like a stalk of wheat, sometimes the 8-shaped *pain fantaisie,* or, with *pâté,* one of the very thin *ficelles*—but otherwise, my irregular loaf, with a bulge on one side or the other (sometimes too burned) has to be weighed, wrapped in paper with a little twist, to put on the back seat of my car and, back at home, on my old thick plank. I may take one back for Janet. Tata likes the *gros pain,* more economical, and it is baked every day for sure.

This afternoon, I have promised to go on an expedition. Three of us are setting out, the other two having lived here longer. I am the neophyte, and that is fine with me. We are on the hunt for the perfect goat cheese, the *fromage de chèvre* you can get in all shapes and donenesses: dry, half-dry, or fresh; it may be covered with crumbs for melting in a salad, or covered with ash for keeping, or then set in fragrant little lumps in a jar with olive oil and fennel seeds. . . . The Jas de something or other which was supposed to furnish the be-all-to-end-all of goat cheeses we were looking for was on the other side of La Roque de Pernes: easy to find, you just take the first turning to the right after the tree with the half-burned trunk, you know, and then, three lanes after, you go halfway to the apricot trees, turn left, go over the hump, turn right again, go past the little heap of stones, and there you are. Can't miss it. My friends had heard of it from a gourmet friend of theirs, and we were bound to find it, they said: *ça vaut le détour,* and is probably worth a whole trip anyway.

"Just past the graveyard,"

we are told, by a glorious blond bathing-suited Wagnerian-type hero.

In the cherry trees behind the cabanon

Part of the present-day cabanon

Vegetables at the Bédoin market

The "meuble" in the kitchen, from L'Isle-sur-Sorgue

ABOVE *Kitchen wall with red casserole and wooden platters*
BELOW: *Cheese stall at a typical market*

The upstairs table under grapevines

ABOVE *Malcolm's vineyard and the Mont Ventoux*
BELOW: *Mormoiron from afar*

At Entrechaux, to get olive oil from the mill

"We eat them all the time, *rien d'autre*,"

he said, and started enumerating how long you could keep which ones.

We went on:

> "*Ah*," said my French companions to me, who knew how long you could keep which ones already, "*vous allez bien aimer le fromage de chèvre.*"

Since I had been coming to France for forty years exactly, and living here for a rather long time, I knew I already liked it. I hate being told what I am going to learn about when it is something I already know, and, still worse, to be told what I am going to like when I already have liked it, dammit.

Down a precipitous stony road with all its stones loose we hurtled, wandered around the chaotic mass of building, and found ourselves in a cool room with the strong smell of goat and that of their product, stronger still. Through a window nearby, the sight of many goats indeed, munching happily on something or other. I would happily have munched on something or other too, but we had to do the round of choosing, complimenting, discussing types of this and that and weather and places with the lovely girl, a braid down her back dark, like Kate Croy the penniless charmer in James's *The Wings of the Dove*. Reeling in the odor, I wasn't taking it all in. My mind was floating away, I had to get it back again—think of the goat smell, what relation to the cheese? look at the way the locket fits so perfectly just between the straps of the sundress of Sylvaine, my friend and guide with the sharp kind face, look at the perfectly groomed hair of my other companion (done by Michel de Crillon, I could tell at a glance), think of something else. No, think goats. Just think: don't faint or wander.

> "I'll take three of this little one to the side, from yesterday, for my supper tonight. Or perhaps one *cendré,* and two of these. When should I serve this one?"

It was like choosing melons: I used to be completely flummoxed when the melon lady would say:

> "Is this for noon or tonight? Or will you be wanting to keep it until tomorrow?"

and continue with instructions about how much sun to give it if I wanted to serve it tonight, and where to put it if it wanted to wait for two or three days. Actually, I just wanted a melon or two, and would figure out later when it would appear on the table. In France, you are supposed to know precisely when and for whom you are doing precisely what. Me, I figure all that out as I go along, very unFrench.

One hour and forty-five minutes later, each of my companions is armed with different-shaped small rounds and squares of cheese wrapped perfectly in translucent paper ("this for tomorrow, this for my nephew—maybe I will have half of this one for supper . . .") are really happy. Nothing puts you in a better mood, if you are French, than going a long way to get a small perfect thing. When there are several perfect things, that is worth the detour, the trip, and everything else.

Yes, It Rains in Provence

When I go over today to see Tata, past her fig tree heavy in the rain, past the old cars rotting in her yard, I remember those tables for the *méchouis* a few years ago, now gone. It is July 10, and it has been pouring every day since May 5, I am told. All I know about it is the cherries rotting on the trees by my cabanon, and the universal laments:

> "How do you expect to sell any cherries with
> all this pourriture? A mess, a mess."

It is all heavy, with the branches hanging down from the trees onto the light bamboo sticks that serve as shelter from the sun, the children's hair drooping into their eyes, and the collective heart of the Vaucluse mourning its customary brightness, seemingly lost forever.

"Summer's not coming this year. Bernard's toothache won't go away."

"Looks like the algae are eating up the lake again. No point in getting poisoned."

There seems to be no other topic of conversation. This one suffices.

My visitor, Tana Matisse, has gone off to see the red and ochre clay cliffs of Roussillon, and the vine-covered houses. She returns by the *Col de Murs*—a narrow road between high rocks which we take as a picturesque adventure, where the view plunges down into the gorges—two hours late and laughing. The village flooded, she asked to borrow an umbrella from a teashop to make her way toward her car, and the *garçon* dislodged one of the massive sun umbrellas to shield her: soon, all the village children were trooping along after her, like René Clair's film *Le Million,* from which I remember only the snaking procession of villagers winding around, smiling.

We go to see my colleague Chris's courtyard, where his neighbor Eugène has put purple and pink flowers in clumps, carefully explaining which flowers take more room for their roots and which can take the shallow flowerbeds or *platebandes* with the old stones underneath. Chris has followed his suggestions, and planted a sweep of colors, startling even in the downpour. Eugène and I go to have a look.

"PUTAIN!" cries Eugène. *"PUTAIN! Ce que c'est beau!"*

In one corner of the old wall, a bedraggled-looking green vine is exhaustedly climbing up as best it can. Chris looks at it, looks at us, and raises his eyebrows inquisitively.

"Ah," says Eugène.
"Ah," he repeats emphatically.
"Ah, quoi, Eugène?"

Smiling conspiratorially, Eugène settles down for a real piece of advice.

"Don't want that plant, right?"
"Of course not."

Chris shakes his damp hair. The rain has not stopped for one second: I have just heard on the radio that it is hailing in Avignon. Well, says Eugène, you just carve a little cross-notch in the central root, put in some hydrochloric acid, and pretty soon, no plant.

"See, if you don't like your neighbor's tree hanging into your yard, anything like that, and pretty soon, it just gets sick and dies."

I look at Chris, who is looking at the ground and the long ash hanging from his cigarette.

"I see," he says slowly. "Time for a pastis."

We talk trees. I tell them about the time my cousin planted a tree behind my cabanon next to the vines. One evening shortly thereafter, the vines' owner, a tall, handsome, and courtly gentleman on a tractor, slowly ran over it with his eyes full on my cousin.

"Didn't have room to turn around," he said. "Sorry, had to," he said.

My cousin picked up the small felled trunk and just stood there, tears in his eyes. What to recount of that? That's just the way it had to be, I guess. Both of them doing what they had to do.

I haven't planted any trees in its place, remembering.

"Provence is not all sunny,"

says the new plumber who has come to fix my water heater.

"You know that, why don't you write it? Tell it like it is."

I guess I will. Some day.

FAMILY AND QUIET TIMES

When we were here all together, for so many years, I already knew how cooking certain things mattered, making somebody's favorite something for some reason or none at all. Just something you could do. Whatever the times are like, you give, said Char, the signs of hospitality to those who come to your door: salt, bread, and water.

The poor man, he used to say, knows how to draw eternity from an olive. In winter time, when my Provençal neighbors Serge and Alain were young, they ate only hot water poured over bread at night. The classic *panade,* bread soup, was made in better times with broth. The sandwich all the Spanish peasants took into the fields at lunch, crusty bread rubbed with garlic, moistened with olive oil, and perhaps a tomato by the side, with salt. Special things were special: Serge and Alain had perhaps a lemon and an orange for Christmas.

You share what you have. Living here is about simplicity. It's about not being more complicated than what you love. I love my neighbors, my cabanon, and how we live right there, when my former husband and I went our separate ways, I remarried. In the winter, we live in New York; in the summer, here. The residents of the cabanon may change, but I have felt part of these walls for a long time, whether I am with a companion or alone.

À TABLE!

"Come over early to eat," say Alain and Geneviève.

"To eat"—in Provence, this can mean lunch or supper, or even breakfast. It is not necessarily broken down into its time-marked components. But it marks friendship like nothing else. In Paris, we would have our *petit déjeuner,* our *déjeuner,* and our *diner,* whereas here, with our farming neighbors, we have our *déjeuner,* our *dîner,* and our *soupers*—since the main meal is at lunchtime. And we were invited early for *souper.* "Early" was for a reason. Alain was going to roast the tiny thrush he had shot over a spit, and they have to be eaten immediately, without reheating. They come in three sizes, the tiniest being the tastiest, which you eat bones and all: as he tells me the names, it sounds something like *la tourche, la quine,* and *le chacha* or *la siffleuse,* the whistler. . . .

As we are having a glass of *suze,* that bitter artichoke liqueur, and gossiping, the little birds are turning over and over, with the *petit salé* between them. Alain would rather have used thin slices of lard, but none was available today: it melts into the flesh and keeps it moist. He tells us the saga of hunting them. Only in Provence, and then during specified times: this is the way it used to be. From September 15 to October 15, you may catch them living, on stakes . . . from January 15 to February 15, you may not move around to catch them, but you may hunt *au poste,* that is, from a shelter, taking living thrushes in cages—*"les appelants,"* to call the others.

We look at a short film his son-in-law has made about him in his film class—"A Rural Life," it is called. Alain on his tractor, smiling in the vines, spraying, trimming the cherry trees, leaving for the hunt with the cages for the thrush, Alain in all seasons.

"A table, à table!"

When we are settled down at the table, he serves first great platters of thinly sliced eggplant, sauteed in olive oil: half are dipped in egg, the others not. He has made a spicy tomato sauce to go with them, and we make our way through what seems fields of eggplant.

"Alain, you don't put garlic in your tomato sauce?"

"Doesn't keep. I'd rather have it taste of thyme than garlic. Like lamb: *il faudrait le piquer avec du poivre vert, pas avec l'ail.* You should season it with green pepper, not with garlic."

About the thrush, says Boyce, "Words are inadequate." He grins; me too. He is quite right. They are served with the sliced baguette they have dripped into, and a salad of *frisée*.

Geneviève has made *sorbet à la poire* and a *sorbet à la framboise,* the flavors of pear and raspberry mingling with that of the hot chocolate sauce poured over them, sticky and runny at once. Alain has made a recipe inherited from his grandparents, of *oreillettes:* thin crunchy pastry, flavored with some *marc de fond* he has saved from the cave cooperative: he gives me a taste, and it puts every other marc I have ever had to shame, or, rather, in the shadow. It used to be that all the grape-growers had the right to a liter every year, but the government has now withdrawn the right. We talk about farming:

"They want everything to be ecological, beautiful, and free of worms. Impossible. Someone asks me about it—I say, fine. I won't use any chemicals, and you sell the produce, with its worms. Okay?"

"What a meal," says Boyce.

Next week Alain's whole family will come to our cabanon—it feels like my family too. My little car bounces quite differently going home late that night.

OLIVES AND IVY

Yes, I remember. When we first came, there was an ivied corner, with the sunlight beaming down on the green . . . then stone stairs were put in, so we could get to the second level, where the peasant keeping the horse for the fields took his siesta. Now there is bare stone for a wall, and the olive grove is gone. Things change around the cabanon, to be sure, but it holds its place, and ours.

One solitary olive tree I planted in the upper field to replace all the lost trees downstairs, and chose it to be right in front of my table, so I could see it right off and always. My friends the classicists declaimed Greek and Latin odes around it, and Tata came to pray at its foot, atheist though she be—"olive trees always bring fortune to everyone," said she, smiling broadly.

My children arrive for a visit, in the early afternoon. We all stand for a long moment in the road, looking at our cabanon that has endured in spite of things. The sky has that whitish blue it takes on in the afternoon, a light breeze is blowing, one of the thirty-four Provençal winds which is neither the mistral nor the sirocco, and the weather is perfect for a walk on the Ventoux.

Early this morning I went to swim in the lake covered with fronds, and placed my espadrilles wet from my putting them on too hastily afterwards upon the low tile roof upstairs, high enough, I hoped, for the neighbor's dog not to find them; I was wrong. I put on my other pair, reminded Hilary and Matthew where they could come across some, in the little trunk where I have always kept bathing suits, sweaters, and extra espadrilles of all sizes. They choose well together: a pale lavender pair for Hilary, and a blue one for Matthew, and look decidedly happier so shod.

It is not a day without accidents. During the night, one of the neighbor's cats must have jumped through the mesh of my tiny kitchen window, knocking everything over, smashing one of the Barroux potter's little dark-green bowls, and littering the floor with tarragon mustard. I have cleaned it up, and am celebrating the children's arrival with my most powerful espresso.

In the glad rush of serving it on the little table outside where they are sitting with the leaves making a dappled light overhead, I knock it off the burner of the gas stove on which it was perilously balanced, all over my wrist and arm. Remembering I have brought some Apinol with me for just such occasions—magic essence of pine tree, from the deep South I sometimes long for—I pat it on the reddening parts of me, and wait. Nothing happens, except the burn worsens.

Hilary and I drive down to the village pharmacy, where they bind me up with compresses and gauze and tape. Leaving, we meet Serge, who inquires what all this is about and sighs:

> "Ah, you could have seen a *guérisseur*—he would have only had to touch the burn, and it would have fled."

Next time, I say, next time I will consult him.

In the special exaltation of minor physical pain, I see the sky oddly as we set off for our walk, driving up through the vegetation growing sparse to the path we will be taking. I don't mention the vipers loosed on the Ventoux to Hilary and Matthew: they may have forgotten one of the peculiarities of the Vaucluse. Even now, these early times stay with us, the times at home and the times spent in nearby places.

"Remember," Matthew says to me, "Remember,

Mummy, when the harpist's score blew away in the theatre at Orange?"

Oh, I do.

"Remember when the black dog at the corner going down leapt out at me, on the back of your mobylette?"

How frightened I was, as I had been so many times going around on my little bike. Sometimes it would refuse to go up hills, just as some large creature would find my ankles appealing for a little nibble . . .

"Remember," Hilary asks. "Remember, Mummy, when everyone in Marseille started fights in the street when the sirocco was blowing too hard?"

Indeed I remember the sirocco, deadly hot, from the desert, but it was all part of the adventure of those first summers. . . .

We talk of the landscapes we remembered: the place we called "The End of the World," high on the mountain, where we would go at twilight to look over the forests and down to the lake. The Dentelles de Montmirail at dawn, with the sun just coming up between the jagged gray peaks. Entrechaux, with its high ruins, or the bareness of Les Baux so deserted and reminiscent of a past you could feel everywhere in Provence, but especially haunting there. We had our *goûter* in the afternoon's fading light: bitter chocolate and faintly sweet Lu biscuits, with a bottle of chilled Deaumes de Venise in a cooler. Why ever go down the mountain? we wonder.

Mainly because of the cabanon. Because of the melons on the bootscraper above the basil plants, against the ochre wall, the apricots in a glazed bowl inside on the yellow oil-cloth, next to the lemon, and the tomatoes, ripe in the earthenware dish. Because this is the place to be together. Or alone. We lay out on the stone steps—still far too steep   our supper, and put a candle on the table.

We are having my **Poulet à l'estragon,** this chicken I have baked with the tarragon I have grown upstairs, a bit of ham and a whole onion in its crevasses, surrounded with tiny irregular potatoes to soak up the juice and the splash of olive oil I had added for flavor. In the other *doux-feu,* I have prepared the thinnest green beans, with olive oil, a bouquet garni, and a cut-up onion, together with a little dash of the dry white wine I am serving, with only a little water inside and a little in the hollow top of the *doux-feu,* so that the inside will remain moist. They have absorbed all the flavor of the oil, and look lovely beside the chicken, on a little green glazed platter from a potter in Goult. To their side, I place some bright tomato slices, interleaved with onion slices, to which we each add a few leaves of the basil plant, dull green and fragrant.

We have time. Later, we will stretch out some sleeping bags and blankets upon the ground upstairs under the stars, bluish-white. Matthew has brought with him a cassette of Mahler's *Das Lied von der Erde,* and the voice of Kathleen Ferrier singing "The Song of the Earth" carries deep and resonant all the way to the cherry trees at the other end of the field. I have put up my gardening tools, and things are quiet now.

MARRIAGES AND MARKETS

CHURCH AND VILLAGE

For occasions such as weddings, funerals, and baptisms, the church/state—or in this case the church/village—relationship comes to the fore. The first time, as I was preparing to go into the church for the wedding of Ghislaine, the daughter of Tata and Jean-Marie, I couldn't figure out why so many men of the village were standing around in the street outside. I asked Laurent, who sold us the cabanon:

"Oh, I never go into the church. I wait here."

And so he did, surrounded by others. If you aren't religious, you just stand outside the church, as a matter of principle. No one minds: this is expected. Many men, in particular, stand around chatting, and wait for the people inside to come out. The invitations read, after the announcement of the marriage by the parents: "*Et vous prient d'assister ou de vous unir d'intention à la Messe de mariage. . . .*" If you choose not to attend, you can still join in the thought of the service. This seems to me an elegant way of treating the problem, which serves as a topic both serious and humorous.

The same occurs with funerals. Serge tells me that in one village, ninety per cent of the inhabitants are non-churchgoers, but, at the moment of the funeral, ninety-eight per cent seem to be, and the crowd outside the church is always larger than the one inside. This is the same village where the farmer going to spray his vines chooses to go at the moment when the others do, a village of convention, or so my neighbors would have me believe. They are perhaps correct. The tradition of participating in the service and in the feelings connected with it outside the church is as firmly entrenched as the collective repast, large or small, following the service.

I went to another wedding in my neighbor's family, this time for the son of Alain, Serge's brother, the one who rescued Matthew when he fell off the wall. It is one of those weddings where the bride and groom give each friend a bottle of wine with their picture reproduced upon it, and a little packet of *dragées,* sugared almonds in pink and white wrapped in a bit of gauze. When you have drunk the wine, says Alain, you make sure to put some dark liquid in the bottle again, before using it as a candleholder. The picture lasts forever. So will the marriage, I expect. We set about drinking the bottles with the picture of the last couple in the family who got married, last year it was, and there they are, untouched by time, fixed forever in the glass.

We celebrate the marriage around a large table, where

much of the village seems gathered. Many toasts, many songs: each of us is supposed to sing something, as is always the tradition at rural feasts in France. It must have taken courage for my children to share in this collective enterprise of neighboring over these years. It is hard enough for me. Not to be a stranger has its requirements together with its privileges, and both of those require participation.

GOATS WITH SIX LEGS: MÉCHOUIS NEXT DOOR

"Will you be here in late August?" asked Tata next door, smiling broadly.

"Yes," I said, "certainly." "*Bien sûr, pourquoi?*"

"You see," said Tata, "it is our turn to have the *méchouis* at our house."

"Yes?" I said expectantly, having no idea what this meant.

It can't be bad, like a sickness, or she wouldn't be wearing that expression. I wondered if it was a celebration, or something to eat. It is, of course, both, like so many things here. They are intimately linked, celebrating and preparing food, enjoying and serving. How it mattered that we be there for whatever it was, next door.

"It will be happening at twelve or one or two,"
said Tata, "Saturday of next week. Just any time
you come over."

The day before, there was a continuous noise of hammering and laughter. The spit was being prepared, the lamb was being prepared, we were all being prepared. About the lamb, though, it turned out there was too little of it for the masses of people expected to arrive. So they had added, as Serge came over to tell me, an extra half-lamb: there would be not four legs, but six to this lamb. And it all had to be placed on the same spit.

As to how many people were finally assembled there, I could not begin to say. Many, including the mayor of Blauvac, the tiny town up the hill from us. The mayor, a great friend of Jean-Marie's, is a superb hunter, and perhaps he is also the mayor. I can't remember, but do indeed remember that it was there in that tiny church that René Char got married three months before he died.

The extremely long feast began with tiny shrimp fritters, Chinese style, that blow up when you fry them. And it ended with all sorts of ice creams. In between, the lamb with its many legs . . . and everything else you could think of. Jokes, songs, tales . . . by six o'clock, we had a longing to return to sleep off some of the rosé wine. Kissing the people we know (as many times as possible on these occasions) and shaking the hands of the others, all four of us trudged back across the neighbor's ground, by the fig tree, through the brambles, down the little path to our cabanon. Three of us collapsed in horizontal positions.

Not Matthew. About two hours later, he came to wake us all.

"Time for rinsing," he says.

"Poor old Matthew," I say sleepily. "Got it wrong. No dishes, no rinse. Goodnight, buster."

"Oho, Mummy. Daddy. Next door. Rinse out the tummy. Onion soup. Tata says you have to come for the rinsing."

We dragged ourselves to a relatively upright position, leaning a bit to the left, took Matthew's hands, quite grubby, but very dear, between ours, nudged Hilary to come along, and returned.

"See there," says Tata, laughing. "Never leave a *méchouis* without rinsing. Bad luck. Night-mares. You have to clean out the system."

And indeed there they all were, spooning up their

onion soup with cheese and bread and more rosé, chatting happily as if they had not just consumed, two hours previously, a gigantic feast with the entire village.

We joined them. More songs. More jokes. More tales.

It was one of the big learning experiences of my life in the Vaucluse—a surprise with a happy ending. The next few weeks, the long tables in back of their house held a few lingering witnesses of the festivity. There was no rush to end it.

MARKETS, MARKETS

Much of the joy of being part of the countryside, and of living here so long, is easily sharable with visitors, as trips to the various street markets embody the collective spirit of Provence more than any single other thing. When we had visitors to the cabanon, one of the first places I would take them, before any wider exploration, was our own Mormoiron market.

MORMOIRON MARKET

Our very local market, in our own village, has two versions: the small one, on Tuesday, which occupies the little parking space by the fountain and comprises just two stalls that I visit always in the same order. First, the fish stall, where I always ask the fishmonger what I should try next. Will it be fresh anchovies? What is that little gray fish? The larger pink one? How do I cook fresh tuna? It may be a red mullet today if friends are coming. Or a *truite saumonnée,* a salmon trout, all pink. And then the vegetable lady, sharp-tongued. You have to converse with her, while she marks up your purchases on a little slate with chalk, as you thrust them into your large woven basket.

At the large market on Sundays, the entire space by the post office is taken up by flowers, lettuce, jams, peaches, pots of basil, olives, a dried fruit booth, and a large vegetable stall. There, the melon lady sees me coming, and chooses four melons for me for ten euros:

"One for today, three to keep a bit,"

she says, and I thank her and take the melons, telling her that I plan to have the largest one myself for lunch. She still always asks when I am going to serve her very precious products, so I have learned to tell her straight off, and to let her help me choose it. I know some of the procedures, but all the same I am always grateful for her rapid help. Rapid, because she has an eye for the customers behind me, of course. After we have that one for lunch, the other three are to place upon the bootscraper in the sun near the basil plant, to ripen a bit, unless friends are coming, when I will halve them, and pour some Beaumes-de-Venise over the pink semi-circles.

Apt Market

Other markets are far larger than the one in Mormoiron. They take up at least a few blocks, or even a whole town, like Carpentras on Fridays, Pernes on Saturdays, and Bédoin on Mondays. In that case, you must know exactly what stalls you want to visit, or you wear out easily. I am prone to wearing out, unless I start early. I have always loved the sound of the name Apt, and the sight of the town's narrow streets thronging. My favorite *vannier* or basket-maker is here, and all my woven baskets and the circular rope rugs covering my floors have come from his workplace.

Early this week we went with our market baskets full of candied fruits, the specialty of Apt, some locally made cylindrical *gaufrettes,* and an almond and walnut pastry, to visit the Apt church and its double crypt. In the first crypt, there is a simple cross surrounded by stone caskets, and beneath, a similar one, its play of light and shadow evident even though it is deep underground. Through this continuity with its past, the Apt market lives with the memory of the dead, fully but unmournfully.

On our way out, at an antique seller's just past the church, I find a water jug whose side is marked by the *coulée,* the liquid trace of the clay running down wet before its glazing. I buy it, to feel and keep the trace of its making. We are offered fresh orange juice, cool, like the jug, the market and the church. Apt seems to contain ongoing things, likely to hold fast.

CARPENTRAS MARKET

When I go to Carpentras to the market, the fifteen kilometers make it an entire expedition for me. As a mild narcoleptic, I tend to fall asleep at the wheel after a few minutes unless I leave early in the morning and avoid the noon light—this has happened three times already, and I aim for it not to happen again. So I set off early, after a bracing very strong espresso in my favorite coffee maker, the kind you plunge down. I also take along some nougat to chew on: sugar is supposed to help. So does chocolate, but it melts in the hot sun here.

I park far away, in a residential district behind the market itself, so as to avoid the traffic, and start out on my trek, with my straw hat and straw basket, equipped against the sun. Today, on my way to market, my hat blew off and rolled right along its rim to a stop in front of a moving truck. The driver screeched to a halt, smiled broadly, and made a sweeping gesture toward my piece of straw there in the road. I dashed in front of him, waved my hat in thanks, and went toward the market.

Actually, the town of Carpentras always seems to me something of a magic place, with its small winding streets; its Passage Boyer—that very old glassed-in walk with shops on each side—and its superb expanse called simply *Les Platanes,* the Plane Trees, has an unforgettable feeling to it. In the famous pastry shop of Jouvaud, the most celebrated concoction is named after the cathedral. Something of a past grandeur pervades Carpentras even now, and the plash of its stone fountains along its main street, leading from the arch called the Porte d'Orange up past the shutters of Jouvaud to the main square. Nearby is the old hospital, now a museum, the Hôtel Dieu, where I had a few interesting stays, before the opening of the new hospital, less picturesquely called the Pôle Santé.

Profusion marks the Carpentras market experience. On market day, Friday, the stalls will cover almost the whole expanse, with two blocks for the flowers, the dried *immortelles* and all the varieties of fresh ones, before the army and navy relics, the knives, and the jackets. Then come the Moroccans, with their cloths and copper and bright piles of oranges, the stands of Indian dresses, and those stalls filled with all the spices, in little sachets. I always get more of the *baies roses,* the tiny sweet pink peppercorns, imported from Africa, as the sellers never fail to say, to explain the stiff price. Piles of espadrilles, and T-shirts, paella and pizzas, everything in its place you get to know, with the sellers teasing and smiling, and the gypsies in their bright skirts, squatting with their garlic and their lemons.

Here at this stall is where René Char would buy his shirts, here, where he would buy his sandals.

At the sausage stalls I get a sausage: a *petit jésus de Lyon,* and if friends are coming, I will get more, one rolled in *herbes de Provence,* one in black pepper, and some thin sticks with olives or hazelnuts. Next, one of the smaller specialized stalls, for a little half-circle from the Ardèche with green peppercorns, heavy, just fitting into your palm. The sausage man is amused, for I come every week to renew my supply, always with the same kind. I get some hot chorizo sausage with which to flavor soups and stews.

Next for the olives, my favorite stop. I especially like Daniel's stall, but almost any of the olive stalls will do if the line by his is too long. I love the gleam of these stalls with their range of olives in straw baskets, tiny like the *coquilles* and massive like the *calamatas,* with their colors ranging from black to green to reddish, from tiny and black to green and whole, from Nyons and from Nice, plain *nature* on pickled and peppered. I pick out my favorites: the black ones scented with garlic and thyme, and the *vertes cassées aux herbes,* the green ones split apart so the herb flavor will soak in. If I feel particularly adventuresome, I will choose the fiery ones with red pepper, whereas if my mood is quiet, I will just take some green ones with fennel: *au fenouil.* I like having at least three kinds to savor alternately. The *tapenade,* a green version from green olives, and black, from black olives, is kept in a large *grès* pottery container. I take some of each, relishing the shine of the olive mixture, and eager to have a spoonful on a piece of fresh baguette: but that has to wait for home.

From the fish man right to the left of Daniel, I pick up some *brandade,* the cod and potato mixture that comes in natural or garlic-flavored, by far the better. Later, I will give Renate Ponsold Motherwell's recipe for her own. And why resist the raw ham, of which there is usually a bargain piece, including the tougher end? I find such buys irresistible and long-lastingly delicious. Of course, when we are making our way over the Ventoux to Malaucène, I like getting the very most flavorful ham there in the shop to the side, but failing that, any raw ham will do. . . .

I pick up some fresh figs, deep purple, precious and rare, at one of the fruit and vegetable stands, where they take place of pride between the neat piles of tomatoes and heaped-up grapes, and the crates of peaches, yellow and white. I discuss with the melon man how to choose the sweetest ones, hoping I will learn to do this correctly some day: weight, smell, the size of the aureole around the stem, the ease with which the stem pulls off, the way the ridges are clearly defined, the slight splitting open that means full ripeness. There is never time to discuss all that with the melon lady in Mormoiron, with impatient villagers lining up behind me. But this is a patient man and he loves to teach, as I love to learn. Just behind him, I know where there are the tiniest new potatoes, pink-skinned and dainty, and that is where I go next, in my habitual fashion.

Then I head toward the cheeses, always the same stand, Chez Louisette: tempted by the rich "killer" mascarpone, the strange strong *Epoisse*—which I can get also in New York, in a round cardboard container for $18, if I feel nostalgic—and the light *Ma Brise,* soft and indescribable in its little individual styrofoam container, with the cellophane you can hardly wait to undo—and I refresh my supply of the *Bleu de Causses* I am inordinately fond of, as I am of the blue *Fourme d'Ambert.* The *chèvres* or goat cheeses are resting on a bed of rushes; I choose a fresh one, from the Banon region—not much taste but refreshing in its soft texture against the older *chèvres* of which I get two small ones, to vary the platter. I take an aged *Cantal,* a *Salers,* which always reminds me of prehistoric caves, and a bit of *Tomme de Savoie,* for its nutty flavor.

The shopper before me, her keen eyes looking over the selection of goat cheeses, finally makes up her mind.

"How should I keep this one, until my guests come next week? "

The cheese man, full of patience, responds. He is the one

who welcomes me week after week, his kind blue eyes above his gray moustache crinkling up at the corners:

"Ça y était, ce bleu? Was that blue cheese good?"

I thank him, for indeed the *Bleu d'Auvergne* he recommended one day was a miracle.

The fish man shouts about his mussels, heaped up and gleaming black and blue:

"Elles sont bien pleines, mes moules, bien pleines!"
They are really full of meat, my mussels, really full!

When I ask how to cook a little pink-gray fish, he wrinkles up his face with laughter and says,

"But with fire, *charmante dame, avec du feu!"*

With a flame, of course. Everyone joins in his laughter, including me.

But I am always afraid of driving, at any hour. As I weave my way uncertainly back from the market, between the stalls along the narrow street, amid the brightly-colored skirts hanging in the wind and swaying from under market baskets, I am definitely not at ease. An old couple in the small truck ahead, apparently of equal age with them, blocks the traffic, afraid to advance. (How I understand them!) Horns hoot, people gesture grandly and with irritation, and what seems only hours later, we can all move, tentatively, if frazzled.

I am relieved to sink into my straw chair by the table, leaving my groceries to unpack themselves later. As for the taste of the *tapenade,* dark and rich and salty, it has not changed.

BÉDOIN MARKET

It is a glorious Monday. Ah, the chickens you can bring home from this market, where you see them roasting on the spit. Truly incredible. Yellow ones, the variety called *poulet jaune,* or larger free-range, or *poulet de Bresse,* and so many other sorts can be found at the Bédoin market, and some others, such as Pernes. And you can also just get a *cuisse* or thigh. I always take the juice and onions you can reheat if you aren't keeping them warm in the roasting paper. I serve whatever kind of chicken I get with the *ratatouille* I make on top of the stove before I leave for the market: it won't burn in my *doux-feu* with the water I put in the oval slot on top. The Le Creuset one in its bright orange always cheers me up intensely.

I always go to the same chicken man, who, with his head on one side, sees me coming, and is grinning at me, seeing my look of longing. I hesitate between sizes and quantities of chicken roasted on the spit: tiny capons, guinea hens, large chickens grown on a farm, ducks stuffed with onion and herbs, small chickens . . . finally choosing two chickens:

"You had only to say: *un poulet quatre cuisses!*"

One chicken with four thighs. That way, you get two for less.

I remember the *méchouis* next door with the lamb and six legs, like the wedding celebration. Sure enough, I say, "*bien sûr,*" and his grin widens. I'll be back next week, I tell him; and I will.

In the round tin pan held out by the vegetable man, I load some tiny eggplants to toss in olive oil tonight, and a long cucumber to serve with the *anchoiade* I made from a small glass of anchovies in salt, much cheaper than in those little tins, and you get to keep the tiny glass.

"Look,"

said the olive and anchovy market man one Monday, "look what *anchoiade* does to the tummy!" And he was happily smiling at his own paunch.

Those anchovies had a particularly good taste: someone had loved them and treated them right. They shone in their salt, alongside the *tapenade* in its cooling crock, and the rows and rows of olives, and everything else. I couldn't wait to get home, just to make sure the taste was the way it always was.

To the far right, the last and largest stall is reserved for the weekly vegetable man. He likes to try things out on me, and that is delightful. This past week, it went like this:

"Comment trouvez-vous que je vous trouve?"

What on earth does that mean? It seems to say, literally: "How do you think I think you are?" I grin, say something like "Ummmm" with what I hope is a French intonation, to show I know perfectly well of what he is speaking, and purchase the fresh garlic he picked for me and a few tomatoes.

That night, I consult with my neighbors Suzanne and Serge as to what I should have answered:

"Very simple," says Suzanne. "You just say: *Et vous?* "And you?"

I never would have thought of that, to be sure. But I'll try it next week, even if I still don't get it. Suzanne, like all my rural friends, has a precise way of understanding people and things. I feel still a stranger in many ways, more than I would like to be, after all these many years.

L'ISLE-SUR-SORGUE MARKET

For the average stroller, there is a particular joy to be taken in antique markets like the Sunday one at L'Isle-sur-Sorgue, where my furniture purchases for the cabanon were all made. My desk, a bit higher than the ordinary, was once a jeweler's work table before the war; the top has a little semicircular groove around the front, a place to put away the working tools, and a tiny double drawer. The wooden trenchers I keep in the tall *armoire* for serving sausages, cheese, and breads, are all worm-eaten and show signs of loving wear. In the center of the largest is a groove which must have caught the gravy from innumerable chickens and roasts. I use an old trencher with a central blade to guillotine the tops of a heap of beans at once, feeling a contact with those before me who cut their vegetables before serving them, perhaps in just such a kitchen as mine.

After browsing among the antiques, we might go to the green wide part of the river, the *Partage des Eaux* about which Char so often wrote, to lunch outside under the plane trees in Le Pescador, the trout restaurant. First, we help ourselves to the plenteous buffet starting with fish soup (shall I have another helping? Yes, at least another), continuing with the celebrated trout of the Sorgue, freshly caught, of course (you have to choose them from the tank), and ending with three perfect sherbets: pear, pistachio, and cassis. Each is surrounded with a different *coulis,* a freshly made sauce of fruits: lime, lemon, and raspberry, and four tiny slices of lemons and oranges to the side.

After lunch, we take a walk along the wide river, which now looks like something out of a Seurat canvas, with people wading, their trousers and skirts rolled up, a few fishermen, two or three rowboats, and brightly clothed groups of Sunday folk idle in the sun by the Sorgue.

SAULT MARKET

To go up to Sault, you choose between two roads up by Villes: the picturesque *route touristique* along the Gorges de la Nesque, staggering in its plunges and swerves; and a less remarkable but more rapid way to get there, picturesque enough, but tamer. On this road, in 1983, Latin inscriptions were found, once again showing that there are traces of the former inhabitants everywhere in Provence—like the Roman wall by our cabanon, or the Roman road leading down from the chapel on our hill. These are the marks of former locals, and are to be treasured.

The market in Sault began in 1515, and every Wednesday since then it has continued. There are the same stalls as everywhere—herbs of all colors and sorts, cheeses galore, honeys liquid or solidified, with all the herbs and flowers imaginable, cloths bright and made into different sizes, gypsy-type garments—but here the stalls spread out along the road by the café overlooking the lavender fields, through an arch into a lovely square, and up a road crowned by the famous nougat shop, *Boyer*. Like the pastry shop *Jouvaud* in Carpentras and also Avignon, these names resonate the lengths of a meal at which anything from either place is served. Proudly.

But one August, my oldest friend Sarah Bird, visiting from Richmond, had gone with me to visit Angelica Garnett—daughter of Vanessa Bell and Duncan Grant—in Forcalquier, up beyond Sault. We had written together a book on Bloomsbury and France, and had met her and her daughter Henrietta because of that. Henrietta had actually chosen the location of our new olive tree upstairs at the cabanon, which was to replace our old and departed olive grove. We had timed our leaving badly, for it was suddenly a Saturday night, we had run completely out of gas, every hotel was taken, and all we managed to do was to park our old 2CV in the town square, as one kind innkeeper suggested, and camp overnight. Difficult, because there was not really enough room either in the front seat, because of the steering wheel, or the back seat, and it soon grew chilly. The innkeeper brought us two blankets, and we struggled through the very, very long night. The next morning, when we returned the blankets, we were treated to a sumptuous bowl of *café au lait* each, and a *tartine* with lavender honey, with inquisitive faces all around. More even to our astonishment, when we left, the garage keeper, now open for the essential gas we had been lacking, filled our arms and car with lavender, Sault's specialty, as an offering from the village—and we made our way home with that scent all around us, over the Gorges de la Nesque, through the great openings in the rocks, with the lavender fields stretching out everywhere around us.

THE POETRY OF
PROVENÇAL COOKING

REFLECTIONS ON CABANON COOKING

Loving in Secret

She has set the table and brought to perfection
what her love seated across from her will speak
to softly in a moment, looking hard at her. This
food like the reed of an oboe.

Under the table, her bare ankles now caress the
warmth of the one she loves, while voices she
does not hear comment her. The lamp's beams
tangle, weaving her sensual distraction.

She knows a bed, far off, awaits and trembles in
the exile of sweet-smelling sheets, like a mountain lake never to be abandoned.

This book was deeply influenced by the poetry of Provence itself, as well as the poetry of René Char, so clearly the reason we first came to live in Provence. Everything in this book that has to do with cooking is simple, and is based on shortcuts. For instance, there are not eight ingredients in my version of home-made olive paste or *tapenade,* but only four. In addition, the truth is that in my own cooking, I sometimes leave out the less essential things, because I wouldn't want to make a special trip down the hill to get them. Near to hand is a good rule, so I like to pick the herbs I use as near to my cabanon as possible, or near the houses of friends, many of whom have contributed their own recipes to this book.

Everything I cook in my cabanon is based on a few ingredients, among which substitutions are always possible, and it all takes the least amount of preparation time imaginable. I would rather look at the sun on the stones and ivy, or then a tree, than spend a great deal of time inside. So I cut my beans outside, in a very old wooden trough, in which a guillotine-like knife is inserted. I beat or stir whatever I can on the little table outside also, and just in general arrange things differently from the way I would in New York.

Every year of the thirty years and more I have lived my summers in this old stone field house we call a **cabanon,** I would grow increasingly unhappy to think that my Provençal cooking would have to end with the oncoming fall and the transfer back to a city world, in another country than France, for me and many the home of food. Consequently I have learned to make the slight adapting gestures necessary and continue to cook in a city apartment as simply as in my cabanon, with a slight change of herbs: the greengrocer at the corner in New York has to stand in for the herbs in my garden. In Provence, I rarely use anything but heavy cooking pots, a steamer, a *doux-feu,* a stove with an oven, sometimes a blender, and sometimes an outdoor grill. I don't use much more than that in the city, where I have no grill, just a broiler and some pots.

The food in these pages is light and rapidly fixed: five to ten minutes preparation time is the average for these recipes, excepting the one coming from my neighbor's on the left for her traditional *soupe au pistou* done the long way, and the complicated and locally-specific recipe for rabbit in *gelée* from my neighbor on the right. These recipes depend for their success in great part on the visual arrangement, on their ease, and on the freshness of the ingredients, the cook's spirit, and the willingness of all participating to share it.

There is a wonderful Provençal cookbook, *La Cuisinière Provençale,* in which the recipes seem to me, if beautiful in conception, still very complicated. I wanted to present something far simpler, for those who want to take far less time. My cooking enthusiasms go out, unsurprisingly, to Elizabeth David, M. F. K. Fisher, and Richard Olney: I delight in reading their descriptions of food and table and market, of Marseilles and the mountains, and I read them aloud to others and silently to myself.

Another minimal gesture I make here, the self-sufficiency of each recipe within itself, is a response to reading such passages as those so frequently found in wonderful Julia Child: "to make X, turn to page Y, then to page Z, where you find the sauce you will have made from page P...." My eyes glaze over, and the book falls from my hands, just as it does when I read, in some well-meaning but deadly text: "Have you planned to incorporate today the following important foods?" I may have planned to, but I will most surely unplan to upon reading anything that sanctimonious.

All of this preference for speed, informality, and spending time with the mountains or my guests may be a direct product of too heavy a reliance on one of my first loves in the kitchen, and which I still recommend wholeheartedly: *The Busy Girl Cookbook.* In Provence, it isn't the business that takes time: it is, as one of my friends puts it, watching the mountain grow. Or just the light shifting. So this is as much a little book about being as about cooking.

In any case, supposing the reader is of a similar cast of mind, here are some tips. You, for example, might be just like me, the kind of person who reads cookbooks for the style of writing and living, not just for the recipes. Who might read something like this book in the middle of the night, with a mug of something hot, perhaps a milk toddy, the kind we used to drink in the South. Who might want, as I do, to transpose the equivalent of Provence elsewhere. I look at the problem of adaptation as an element of being, remembering *The Joy of Cooking* we and our mothers all used to read, in the tattered edition that our mothers passed on to us. Wanting to pass something on in my turn, about rapid preparation of things that rapidly disappear from the table, I have put together this book, to which my neighbors have so kindly contributed.

N.B.: *In these recipes, the order is more or less alphabetical, according to the principal ingredient, in French. I have made no effort to regularize the styles of the recipes, since very often they have been given to me by my neighbors, and I wanted to keep their cooking voice.*

Hors d'oeuvres et Amuse-Gueules
Hors d'oeuvres, Snacks, and Beginnings

❦

PASTIS TIME

When it is pastis time, the before-supper hour, the gray-blue stoneware jug holds chilled spring water, and a bowl of the same gray-blue holds a few ice cubes. I am serving my beloved *anchoiade,* that strong dipping sauce of anchovies melted with hot olive oil and garlic, surrounded by fennel stalks and small yellow crackers, those Tucs that disappear from the table no matter what you put on them, and also *tapenade.*

Anchoiade/
Anchovy Dip

for which you need just some anchovies from the market, from one of those great vats, or some salted anchovies in a little glass jar. Soak them to get rid of the salt, split them lengthwise in two and remove the tiny central bones. Put them in some good olive oil, as green as possible, in which three or four largish cloves of garlic crushed in a mortar with a pestle have been slightly browned, until they start melting together. Push them around with a spoon, mix all together, and serve hot with carrot and cucumber sticks, celery stalks or fennel root, radishes, raw cauliflower or broccoli, crackers, or anything else to hand.

From my Marseillaise friend:

Marie-Paule's **Anchois aux poivrons/Anchovies with Peppers** which takes one cup of red pepper strips, one-half cup of anchovies, with the bones removed and desalted, and breadcrumbs (*chapelure*). Place the red pepper and the anchovies side by side, and the *chapelure* on top. Bake in a moderate oven, until the pepper is just done, about thirty minutes.

Brandade de morue/
Purée of Salt Cod

We are having a very dry white wine that Malcolm prepared with his daughter Lucy, and a celebratory meal, even though at this point I have totally forgotten whatever it is we are supposed to be celebrating. Is it being together, my excuse when I have no other reason? In any case, and whatever the reason now lost, it matters little now. I am serving a homemade *Brandade,* using the recipe my friend Renate Ponsold gave me. Yes, I could have gotten this in the market, and actually every time I make it think I will next time, but then I am retempted to do it myself:

Renate's Brandade de Morue/
Purée of Salt Cod

For four, you need 1 pound dried salt cod, 3 large baking potatoes, 6 cups unsalted fish stock, 2 crushed garlic cloves, ½ cup extra-virgin olive oil, ½ to ¾ cup heavy cream, and crushed coarse sea salt and freshly ground pepper to taste; then 4 puff-pastry shells. Soak the cod up to 24 hours in cold water, changing the water every few hours. Preheat the oven to moderately hot: 450 degrees (8-9 French gas). Bake the potatoes for an hour, until soft. Cool and scoop out the flesh into a bowl. Drain the cod and discard any skin and tough parts. Cut into small squares and place in a pot. Add the stock and simmer for 20 minutes. Drain, and place in your mortar. Pound it to a fine paste with a wooden spoon or pestle. Add the potato flesh to the fish puree, with the garlic, if desired. Pounding constantly, add the olive oil drop by drop, then the cream. The consistency should be that of a coarse paste. Season with salt and pepper to taste.

Serve hot, scooped into puff-pastry shells, or then just toast triangles, fried in a little butter.

Bruschetta/
Basic Bruschetta, Cabanon Style

Chop a quantity of plum tomatoes, fresh from the market if possible. Combine them with at least 10 good-sized basil leaves from your plant, enough olive oil, and the juice of half a lemon. Then add some crushed red pepper flakes, and marinate for a few hours.

You can serve this on toast rounds, with tapenade on the side, perhaps some green and some black, for the colors. (Always make more than you think you need, because it disappears as if by magic.)

Greg Todd, lawyer and lover of philosophy, is the son of David and Sue, our great friends from the very old village of Venasque. That picturesque village, situated on a high bluff with its eleventh-century crypt looming above the landscape, is just twenty minutes away from Mormoiron by winding roads. Greg is a passionate climber of hills, such as those we have around here, for example, the Dentelles de Montmirail, near the wine villages of Vacqueyras and Gigondas.

Greg's Caviar du pauvre/
Poor Man's Caviar

You just need eggplant, olive oil, garlic, and lemon. Put the aubergines (eggplants) under the grill and char the skin until it is crackly, and can be easily removed. Mash the flesh with olive oil, lemon, and garlic.

Escargots/
Snails

A perfect beginning to any cabanon meal, given the plentiful supply of these delicious beings. Even better when you have guests who do not care for them: more for you.

After any rain, there abound snails of all sizes—you can feel them crunching under your foot down the stone stairs of the cabanon. Early in the morning, whether or not the rain has stopped, the neighbors come to gather them in great pails, smiling widely.

Suzanne explains to me the preparation of snails in Provençal fashion. It takes three days, and you have to starve them, perhaps in the bathtub. You put a branch of thyme near them—they will not eat it, but it perfumes them. You must clean them entirely after three days, then prepare them with parsley and garlic. "*Tout ce travail,*" says Suzanne, then they disappear so quickly.

Gravlax/
Boyce's Gravlax

You will be needing two salmon filets, of the same size. In a bowl, mix ⅓ cup sugar and ⅓ gros sel, with abundant black pepper. Rub some vodka or aquavit into the salmon flesh, then the salt mixture. Place a good quantity of dill weed *aneth* on this.

Place one of the filets skin down in roasting dish, and the other 180 degrees rotated, on the first. Sprinkle the remaining salt mixture over them, cover with plastic wrap or tinfoil, then a dish and at least a five pound weight.

Every 12 hours, invert the filets, for three days.

Then serve, either on some mesclun leaves or well-done toast.

It isn't just being with friends that is such a help, it is knowing they are there. My wonderful Cornish painter friends Clive and Ann, whom I met when they just came, in the late 80's, to live part of the time in Villes, have a way of warming any town they are even near. And often, when I am alone in the cabanon and need comforting, I will make for myself a recipe given me by Ann, a cook beyond measure. For example, her:

Courgettes farcies/
Stuffed Zucchini,

which means covering the bottom of an oiled baking dish with thinly sliced onion, halving some zucchini lengthwise, cutting each half into a fan shape which you fill with sliced tomatoes and place on top of the onion, seasoning with salt, freshly ground pepper, and some whole coriander seeds. Pour in some dry white wine so that it comes halfway up the zucchini. Trickle in a little olive oil, cover the dish with foil, and bake for about 45 minutes.

Tapenade

Green Tapenade: You use masses of green olives, pitted. In Provence, you get them in the market, whereas anywhere unmarket-supplied, you use them any way you can get them: in jars or cans. I would make far more than you think you need of this delicious treasure: the caviar of Provence. Put them in the blender with some very green olive oil, some anchovies in their oil or however they come, and some capers. If you prefer using tuna fish to anchovies, that is fine too. Then you blend, and, voilà, your tapenade is ready.

For **Black Tapenade,** you just use black olives.

> For breakfast, served with *tartines* or toast, nothing is better. I would spread a little black *tapenade* on one crusty piece, and a little green on another. Make that a lot, actually. It's pretty good for lunch too, on a bit of *frisée* lettuce, the black showing up against the green, or, if you are using the green kind, hiding amid the lettuce. If I'm serving something without a lot of color, like *tapenade,* I'll always put something with red peppers next to it, just for the color.

Marie-Paule's **Tapenade aux Aubergines/ Eggplant Tapenade.**

You char the eggplant in the oven, until the skin slides off easily, scoop out the flesh, mix with *tapenade,* and place on toast. Easy. Wonderful.

It is to be served before the meal, with a tiny crock of butter for those who want it, some toasts or crackers, and preferably a good glass of *pastis* of at least 45 degrees, with lots of ice and water. Make that several glasses. You may not need supper; you will need more *tapenade.*

Soupes et Potages
Soups

༄༅

I cannot imagine anything more useful than throwing together what you have, wherever you are, and heating it up. In the cabanon, I use a large orange Le Creuset casserole, which never lets things burn. I just put whatever I have, often potatoes and tomatoes, to which I have added the green top part of some leeks, some thyme and bay leaves from a tree just up by the cabanon of my neighbors to the right, the Amiets (see their recipe for *Lapin au basilic*). At the last moment, I add a little milk. It is an improvised *soupe aux poireaux*.

I also love cold soups, and make them often, with yogurt and cucumbers and dill, or then zucchini and fennel. Many of the following soups can be served hot or cold—since I often have no idea how many guests will be dropping in for a meal, that turns out frequently to be soup.

In our family, I would take turns with each person's favorite things; I had a turn too. Avoiding, of course, the three things each of us got to choose to hate. Reluctantly, then, I would occasionally give up serving eggplant, say, or anchovies, the way in New York I would (sometimes) give up serving things with ginger. We each had privileges of likes and dislikes. Cabanon family life is not all that different from any family life.

And then there were celebrations. Mostly of the small kind, because I figured the large occasions could take care of themselves. I would want to celebrate Hilary's feeling that she had finally got down her hardest piece for her recorder, or Matthew's new song for his guitar, or their newly discovered insect pet, something like that. These were excuses for gladness, for which any excuse should do. Me, I most love making soups, vegetables, and desserts. So a celebration of being just with family for me may consist of my serving exactly those things, in the cabanon or elsewhere. You will hear enough of my soups: I make any soup with joy. Just give me a chance.

Carrots and leeks go wonderfully together, so I sometimes make a combined

Potage Carottes et Poireaux/
Carrot and Leek Soup

I would make this with carrots and leeks, using three or four leeks, four or five good-sized carrots, about a pound of potatoes, and three or four onions. I wash the leeks carefully and chop all the vegetables in smallish pieces, then place them in a few tablespoons of olive oil in which a clove of garlic has been simmering; the clove can then be discarded. And finally I add water or stock, and let this boil, with some salt, until everything is tender.

This is particularly good if you are expecting leeks and potatoes only, and suddenly you are surprised with a slight orange color. A healthy addition!

Potage de courgettes/
Squash Soup

I love to save all vegetables for soup, especially green ones. You just blend them with a bit of bouillon and curry powder and have a green soup with croutons. This is one of those soups that calls aloud for a dollop of *crème fraîche* and of course a good deal of freshly ground pepper. And I always keep my basil plant on the table handy, for anyone to take some sprigs to put in the soup.

I always make soup, even when it is a scorcher—I love soups both hot and cold. For instance, since I love watercress for its bitter distinctive taste, one of my favorite soups is a

Potage au cresson/ Watercress Soup

You wilt a bunch or two of watercress in a lump of butter, browning it slightly, tossing a few onions about in the same butter, and several potatoes finely diced. Then when it is all a bit glazed, you add about three cups of water. When it is all feeling tender, you put it in the blender very briefly (avoiding mush), and return it to the fire for just enough time to reheat it. You might want to place a little bowl of croutons sauteed in olive oil and herbs and garlic alongside this: I always do, for its texture. You can toss them in butter if you prefer—I prefer olive oil, for the nutty flavor—but in either case let them brown at least slightly. More taste.

Casserole des haricots/
Boyce's Bean Stew
(liberally adapted from Cook's Magazine*)*

- 1 lb beans—of several sorts and sizes, the cook's choice
- 3 tbsp. olive oil
- 1 to 1½ lb. chorizo or any available hot sausage, skinned and chopped as finely as possible
- 1 large yellow onion, chopped into ½ inch pieces
- 2 stalks celery, chopped into ½ inch pieces
- 2 carrots, chopped into ½ inch pieces
- 3 garlic cloves, chopped finely
- 1 qt stock
- A cup diced tomatoes, or 1 large tin of diced tomatoes
- 3 cups water (using water from tinned tomatoes, if you used a can)
- 2 bay leaves
- ½ head cabbage, in ½ inch pieces
- Rosemary or tarragon, freshly ground pepper, and salt

Salt enough water and use it to soak the beans overnight. Drain and rinse. In a pot, add 1 tbsp. of the oil and the garlic. Add the sausage, and cook until it loses its pink color. Remove to a dish covered with paper towels. Add 2 tbsp. of oil to the pot, and add the onions, celery, and carrots; cook with low heat for 10 to 15 minutes until well softened. Stir in the stock, beans, water, bay leaves, and bring to simmer. Then place in the doux-feu and simmer for 45 min., on top of the stove or in the oven, being sure to keep enough water in the hollow on the top. Then stir in the cabbage, tomatoes, and sausage, and bring back to a simmer. Cook for 40 min. or so. Do not let the beans get mushy.

> Serve with a dollop of sour cream. Serves 8. We would serve this as a simple supper, with a green salad and cheese. A slightly chilled light red wine is best with it, the cool glass making a good balance with the hot soup. A perfect dish for a cabanon, or just about anywhere, inside or out.

Crème de Navets/
Cream of Turnip Soup
Adapted from Les Secrets de la Bonne Table

Peel about a dozen turnips, cut them in rounds, throw in boiling water and take off the stove. After five minutes, strain, rinse, and drain the turnips. Heat them in a bit of butter (one-eighth of a cup), add 2 pints of milk, salt, mixed spice, and white pepper, cover the pan, and when the turnips are tender, mash them through a colander.

> This is an unusual soup, but, for that very reason, I find it delightful to serve. I sprinkle sprigs of cilantro or Italian parsley over it to give it some color.

In the evening, if I am alone, I put out my dinner on the tall stone steps, take up Colette's book *Break of Day*, about her living in a cabanon in the Midi, and settle down to my soup in a yellow bowl from the enormous black tureen, place my *ficelle*—narrower than a baguette, more crust— on the heavy cutting board, and keep my basil plant nearby to help myself from. Some evenings, I make just for myself the very simple

Potage à la passoire/ Leftover Soup,

where you put anything you have left over through a food mill (or into a blender), adding some beef or chicken stock, and I might use two or three pounds of tomatoes and one-half that amount of potatoes, put them through a vegetable sieve (the *passoire*), cook them in the stock with the leftovers, add some fresh basil and a dollop of cream.

Soupe au Pistou is the famous Provençal soup of vegetables, pasta, and pesto: very garlicky and thick.

And Janet's pistou, different from Suzanne's, is equally good. Both take great quantities of time and vegetables, but Janet's has the *pistou* in it and Suzanne's puts it on the side, so you can take as much as you like. (I like a lot.)

Janet's Pistou

calls for: onions, tomatoes, three kinds of beans, squash, leeks, carrots, pine nuts, and sometimes pasta. She cooks some chopped onions in olive oil until they are soft, adds two or three peeled tomatoes, chopped, and a good bit of water. When it boils, she adds white beans, green beans cut up in small lengths, red beans, and an assortment of other vegetables cut up smallish, like leeks and zucchini. She cooks them slowly in enough water, adds two or three tomatoes at the end of the cooking, and adds, before serving, her *pistou,* a fragrant and powerful sauce of olive oil and garlic pounded and mashed with a mortar and pestle, to which are added ground pine nuts and at least 8 large springs of basil.

> The *pistou* around a table makes an entire evening, served with rosé wine, or white, with sliced melon first and a salad. I always feel in a good mood when it is announced.

PISTOU AROUND A TABLE

Suzanne's cuisine is celebrated: she can make subtle dishes from many regions, but she can also cook Provençal dishes with the gusto they require. She works hard at whatever she cooks—nevertheless, to make the famous dish of Provençal *pistou,* she works even harder. The three kinds of beans, none from a tin, the tiny tomatoes and carrots . . .

> *"J'ai aidé, moi!"* says her daughter Lydie, seven and always smiling. "It's so good because I helped."

Now Suzanne's *Pistou* is a true production, and I will give her recipe as she gave it to me, for six persons. This production is a perfect example of cooking with love, in Provece.

Suzanne's Pistou

three and a half cups of white beans and red beans each; two and a fourth cups of green beans; one and three-fourth cups of carrots and turnips each; two medium green zucchini; one leek; an entire head of garlic; two plum tomatoes; one little sachet of parmesan cheese; two-thirds of a cup of elbow pasta; a glass and a half of olive oil (you can use the light or yellow kind, if you fear the *pistou* will be too rich); the leaves of three branches of basil; salt and pepper to taste.

Prepare the white and red beans; peel and cube the carrots and turnips. Snap the ends off the green beans, and put all of this in a large casserole or pot. During this time, heat the water with salt. Continue peeling the zucchini, and the leek, and cube them when the beans have been cooking for a half an hour. Put the zucchini with the leeks, and let them cook for a good hour. Fifteen minutes before the end of the cooking time, add the whole unpeeled tomatoes, and then at the last minute, remove them.

Add the pasta, and make the *pistou:* peel the tomatoes and put them in a bowl, mashing them with a fork and adding the garlic, basil, and the parmesan cheese. Mix well and add the olive oil little by little, still stirring. Salt and pepper as you like. Serve the soup hot and the *pistou* on the side, so each one can put as much as is desired in the soup. This soup can be prepared easily in advance but without the pasta, which would get soggy. Put that in 5 minutes before serving time.

There has always been a special magic about *pistou,* and I have never met anyone immune to it. Thankfully, its mystique survives intact, throughout the years. It knits friends and families together, and—for all the effort it requires—is the greatest soup imaginable, fully worth every moment of preparation. It is usually quite enough for dinner, with some rosé wine and crusty bread, and perhaps a salad.

> "You won't get over it soon," Serge to me. "If I want my guests to drink a lot, I add more pepper and more garlic. If not, presumably, not."

We pass around an extra bowl of pine nuts and basil and garlic made liquid with olive oil:

> *Attention,* they say, *cela donne* soif.

Indeed it does make you thirsty, and bottles of chilled rosé are welcome. You stagger home, happy.

Tina's Soupe aux Poireaux et pommes de terre/ Leek and potato soup

While I would be talking to René Char, Tina would be sauteeing chopped onions and leeks in olive oil to translucency, then adding diced potatoes and stirring them about before pouring the water over them to simmer until the potatoes are tender. At the end, she would mash it all together to make it creamy. . . . But you could just leave the elements loose like that.

This has always been my idea of a perfect soup to serve when you have no time.

Soupe aux Pois Chiches/ Chickpea Soup
Adapted from Elizabeth David's French Country Cooking

Soak a pound of chickpeas in tepid water with some coarse salt and 2 tbsp. flour overnight, and the next day boil the water with a pinch of bicarbonate of soda, cool it, and add the chickpeas again. Simmer for an hour, strain, and place the peas in a large pot of fresh boiling salted water to loosen the skins. Save half, season with olive oil, and serve as a salad (see SALADS).

In a saucepan place a sliced onion and two chopped leeks, and a chopped skinned tomato. Simmer the other half of the peas in the same water, and serve with *croutons*.

I like to add some thin slices of sausage, or left-over beef.

Soupe de poisson à la Marseillaise/ Fish Soup Mode Marseille

Translated from the Cuisinière Provençale, *which calls for two leeks, two onions, some olive oil, two tomatoes, diced, two crushed cloves of garlic, a sprig of fennel, a bay leaf, a piece of orange peel, two liters of water, two pounds of rock fish (little crayfish, crabs, rascasses, eels), a pound of vermicelli, and a pinch of saffron. I give the recipe almost exactly as it reads in the book, knowing this to be a serious and Marseillaise matter.*

Chop finely two leeks and two onions, and put them in a pot with a few spoonfuls of oil until they glaze. Add two chopped tomatoes, leave on the stove one minute, stirring. Add two crushed cloves of garlic, the sprig of fennel, a bay leaf, and a piece of orange peel; wet with two liters of water. Add two pounds of rock fish; add salt and pepper, and cook at a moderate boil for 15 minutes. Place the liquid in another bowl, pressing the fish down into the strainer with a wooden spoon to extract the juices. Return the bouillon to the fire and let it come to a boil. Add a pound of vermicelli and a largish pinch of saffron.

Let it cook over a slow heat, and serve with its *rouille* and croutons and cheese.

La Rouille (the rust-colored mayonnaise, garlicky and peppery, for fish soup)—I am putting it next to the fish soup, lest we forget. It calls for one or two egg yolks, olive oil, two cloves of garlic, and a small hot red pepper. You thicken an egg yolk with olive oil added by drops, to make a good mayonnaise, to which you add two cloves of garlic to make a basic aioli, and then the red pepper, which itself is the *rouille,* making the whole thing a deep rust color, as in the term "rouille."

You make your croutons out of last night's baguette in rounds, toasted in the oven, and put with the *rouille* and a little bowl of grated cheese, and a small bunch of basil on the tablecloth, with perhaps a little bowl of garlic. Each person takes three or four croutons, peels a clove of garlic if desired, to rub on the croutons, puts a dollop of *rouille* upon them, and the cheese over them, and douses the whole thing with the soup so it melts to a delightful stickiness. The basil floats about, intoxicated, like you with the dry white wine you serve. A joy, winter or summer.

Without rouille, fish soup is as a tinkling cymbal.

On cooler evenings, I occasionally prepare a

Potage de poulet au cabanon/ Cabanon-style Chicken Soup

I simply boil some leftover chicken, including the bones (probably from the **Poulet à l'Estragon** we would have had the night before) with whatever greens I might have on hand, and whatever vegetables like carrots, squash, or onions, the more the better, adding fresh basil or dill. Then, at the last minute, when the flavor has developed, you can add pasta—which our children used to like, or then a cup of milk or a little cream. Like many soups, it improves with reheating, whatever additions you prefer.

Potage de Salade/
Salad Soup

*Adapted from Elizabeth David's recipe for **Potage du Père Tranquille** (who was a Capucin monk, and the soup is named also after the soporific virtues of lettuce).*

Take any lettuces you are particularly fond of, two or three, depending on the size, cut into ribbons, and simmer in a pint of chicken broth. Puree in blender, return to the pan, add the milk, a bit of sugar and salt and a grating of nutmeg. Before serving, stir in a bit of butter or *crème fraíche* (sour cream will do).

I find this far more interesting than cold gazpacho, and so sometimes make it with leftover salad, which is just as good if not better. But in that case, forget the milk, use just the broth, and add the cream or butter at the very last moment. Especially useful when you have people staying, so you can use the salad they didn't have room for, in the soup.

Les Oeufs
Egg Dishes

❧❧❧

Tata's Blettes Provençales en Omelette/ Swiss Chard in Omelet

You parboil the whole long green top and the white bottom, then divide each stalk in two. The top you cut very finely and use in your omelet as if it were spinach, and the bottom you toss in a pan with garlic and olive oil, either to serve alongside the omelet or in it, mixed along with the green part. In either case, says Tata, you serve it with a tomato salad, so your plate will look red, yellow, and green.

Omelette aux Croutons, Tomates, et Fromage/ Omelet with Croutons, Cheese, and Tomatoes
Adapted from Elizabeth David's
French Country Cooking

A simple Provençal dish. You just *sautez* little rectangles of bread until they are crisp (I like them very brown), and then put the eggs in the pan in butter, the croutons and diced tomatoes on top, and add a good handful of grated yellow cheese, before you fold it all over. Put a good amount of tarragon on top, or basil if the tarragon has made itself scarce. . . .*

*This happened to us for two summers straight, and we found basil to work particularly well.

Omelette Ratatouille

My neighbor Tata puts her omelet and her *ratatouille* together, and adds some streaky bacon—called *petit salé*—or *poitrine fumée,* or whatever little ham bits she has left and kept for just such a purpose. This is perfect, accompanied by fresh rosé or dry white wine, a green salad, and a plain crusty *baguette.*

Oeufs pochés/
Provençal Poach

For breakfast, we like eggs poached like this: we add 2 inches of water to a pan sufficiently deep to cover the eggs. Add a little vinegar to the water and bring it to a slow boil. Then break each egg into a small bowl and pour it carefully into the simmering water: two at a time can be cooked, but the water has to stay at a near boil. Lift out the egg with a slotted spoon, touch the bottom of the spoon to a towel to dry it off, put the egg on toast, salt and pepper it, and place some basil leaves around it on the plate.

This is a perfect dish to carry outside in the early morning. If you are feeling energetic, a few slices of broiled tomatoes are a great addition.

Poissons
Fish

꧁꧂

Bourride/
Bourride

Here's the good thing about this recipe—you DON'T have to use any particular kind of fish, just whatever you find in the market—so it is unlike bouillabaisse with its required this and that.

You make the *court bouillon* very simply: some fennel (you will have had some to serve with anchoiade or then with tapenade, and you can just use the amount you feel like using or happen to have), an onion, lemon peel, bay leaf, and the usual salt and pepper, a splash of white wine, AND the fish heads you've taken off or had taken off (in which case, remember to ask for them, and the bones, which are useful for your fish soup). Simmer all that for a quarter of an hour, strain it, and let it cool. Then put in the fish you chose and bring it again to a simmer until they feel done.

You will need to make an *aioli,* always fun. (Crush 3 cloves of garlic, add 2 egg yolks, half a pint of olive oil, and lemon juice to taste.) Half of it goes in the top part of a double boiler, to which you add 4 beaten egg yolks and a ladle of the court bouillon, and reheat it while stirring with a whisk. Put this over toasted French bread (of course) in a serving dish, with the fish on top. The other half of the aioli is for people to add to the fish once it is on their plate.

I am very fond of making **poisson en papillotte**, which is just fish in tinfoil, rolled up with herbs and onions and whatever else you like. Like a crepe, but different.

You can use any fish you like, but here is a recipe for

Maquereau en papillotte/ mackerel in tinfoil

I took some smallish Mackerel basted with the olive oil Philippe next door gave me, from his olive grove, and some parsley the vegetable lady gave me inside, and sea salt. Then I fold them over in tinfoil, the edges squeezed up like a sort of shell.

I served it with long-grain rice, tossed with olive oil and garlic in my enormous iron pan before any water touched it. To the side, a little heap of very thin green beans I topped outside yesterday, in a daydreaming moment, under the trees with my old wooden instrument, like a guillotine, and then steamed briefly with oil and herbs. A salad of lamb's lettuce with a plate of cheeses makes a perfect ending.

Moules marinières/
Mussels Sailor Style

when I allow myself about three-fourths of a pound of mussels large or small, clean them, place them in a pot with several cloves of crushed garlic, a smidgen of water and a half a cup white wine for each pound of mussels (if I am inviting more people than just me), and cook until they open. I discard any that do not, place a spoonful or two of *crème fraîche* over them, and place them in my plate if I am alone, or, if I have invited others, in a large central bowl, making sure that each person has enough liquid to dip up with the shells the mussels are now resting in, plumply.

Elizabeth David's first encounter with mussels in her childhood bears re-reading, as does all her writing about food:

> One day, Marie came into the dining-room bearing a big tureen of mussels, cooked in some sort of creamy sauce flecked with parsley and probably other garden herbs as well. The appearance, the smell and the taste of those mussels were to me most fascinating and mysterious. The little black-shelled objects didn't seem like fish at all, they had the same kind of magical quality as mushrooms, the real field mushrooms which, as children, we had so often brought home for breakfast after a dawn search in the fields round our home in the Sussex Downs. (*An Omelette and a Glass of Wine,* p. 86.)

I cannot resist adding her first encounter with **Moules normandes**:

> They were cooked in their own liquid until they opened; fresh cream was poured over them; they were sprinkled with chopped fresh

tarragon; and brought to the table piled up in a tureen. Nothing could be simpler; and to us, living so few short miles across the North Sea, not humming birds could appear more magical, nor mandrake root more unlikely. (*An Omelette,* p. 88.)

These were *bouchots* from Brittany—those mussels gathered from wooden stakes—but the joy is transferable to our own mussels, cooked Norman style.

Suzanne's Petite friture/ Little Fish Fry,

which is simply two little handfuls of these tiny fish per person, covered in flour an lightly tossed, dried, and lightly tossed in corn, sunflower, or peanut oil for about two minutes, and sprinkled with dill (*aneth*) or thyme, and half a fresh lemon to squeeze over the little gray fish, and give them color. You serve them IMME-DIATELY, with rosé or white wine, as a first course.

Maybe as a first course, but I remember many times in Venice subsisting on this dish as a perfect main course, followed by a salad as a complete meal. But then I guess the fish were different. . . .

I also love the very simple

Poissons au fenouil/
Fish with Fennel,

which takes one filet of rouget per person, or whatever fish you think appropriate, butter or very green
olive oil, and fennel. You broil or grill the filets rapidly with a little oil or butter on top, with some stalks
of fennel to the side. Serve with rice.

Whenever I have some fish left over, I save it to add as a
garnish to the stock I have made. Like all savers everywhere, I have boiled the fish head and tail with a few
herbs, putting them then in the blender, bones and all in
the cooking water. When I reheat it and add the leftover
fish and a little *crème fraîche,* salt and freshly ground pepper,
I would love to consume it all myself. Sometimes I do,
sometimes I am generous enough to share it.

I love dropping in on Mireille and Michel, who enjoy
making lunch for me and showing me how to prepare
food as simply as possible. This recipe for fresh fish—
Mormoiron on Tuesdays, Carpentras on Fridays—is
simple, to the extreme, and I have made it many times.

Mireille's Poisson Grillé/ Grilled Fish

calls for a clove of crushed garlic, a tablespoon of finely chopped onion, some anisette or a little *pastis,* some juniper berries if you have some, a sprig of thyme, a sprig of rosemary, and a little water to be shaken together. You keep this in a bottle to shake over the fish while it is grilling, then you salt and pepper the fish and serve it with rice and a green salad.

Bottles of seasoning are most useful: I keep also a bottle of ***huile d'olive poivrée*** with red pepper, to sprinkle over any fish served hot or cold.

Alain's Poisson provençal

which takes two carrots, two onions, two bay leaves, a large fish (*daurade* or salmon or trout), and some assorted herbs. Put enough water to cover the fish, with the carrots and onions and a bay leaf, to boil in a fish pan or casserole. Add the fish, bring to the boil, cook three minutes, and let chill overnight in the marinade. The following day, reheat until tender, and serve with freshly made mayonnaise, which I love making, just dribbling the green olive oil over the beaten egg yolks and a little vinegar until it thickens.

Mireille told me how to make

les Rougets grillés/
Grilled Red Mullets.

She uses a few small fish or one large one, and scores the fish across, marinating it in olive oil and a cup or so of white wine. Then she tosses a mixture of chopped fennel leaves with olive oil, thyme, and whatever other herbs she feels like that day, grills it, and serves it hot or cold, surrounded by slices of lemon, or black or green olives, with a few fennel stalks. When I do this, I like to have a bottle of olive oil marinated in fennel alongside. This is good with potatoes, hot or cold, tossed with olive oil, and a green salad, with a dry white wine.

My friend Judith Baker, of St. Hippolyte Le Graveyron, a famous chef, prepares a splendid

Saumon en croûte/
Salmon en croûte

Scarcely a cabanon dish, but irresistible in every way

2x550-g pieces of thick salmon fillet, skinned, each
    being about 20cm long
500g cooked spinach, drained, chopped and
    cooled
2x500-g packages of puff pastry
1 beaten egg
2 tablespoons of cream cheese
Juice half lemon

Trim fillets to same size and season each piece. Remove any bones with tweezers.

Cover one half with half the spinach, the cream cheese, and the lemon juice.

Roll out one of the pastry blocks to roughly the same size as this salmon fillet.

Lift the stuffed fish onto the pastry and season.

Cover with the second fillet and spread the remaining spinach.

Roll out the second pastry block, making it a little larger than the first one.

Cover the fish. Tuck pastry well in around the salmon and seal carefully. Trim excess pastry, making sure the outsides are tightly sealed.

Brush the salmon with the beaten egg and place in fridge for 5 minutes.

Score and decorate the parcel and put into a pre-heated oven (200°C Gas Mark 6) for 35–40 minutes. Remove and leave to rest for 5 minutes.

Cut into thick slices and serve with a sauce of your choice, and a green salad.

Tata gave me a recipe for her

Thon en tranches/
Sliced Tuna,

which calls for a slice of thickish tuna, for two people, and a little olive oil for cooking it just slightly. You throw that oil out. In another dish, put some butter, an onion sliced, a clove of garlic crushed, and some peeled tomatoes. Place these on the tuna, with some fresh basil, and bake for an hour at moderate temperature. Serve with a white wine "of character." You can also grill it and serve it rare, with uncooked tomato slices on the side, which I enormously prefer.

Viandes
Meats

꧁꧂

Poulet rôti/
Lucy's Roasted Chicken

Choose in the market an organic free-range chicken.
Rub it all over with a garlic clove, and place slivers of
garlic in all the crevices. Then smother it in goose fat
and place it in the roasting pan with slices of onion
and some olive oil and white wine. Sprinkle over it
some *ras el-harout,* any available paprika-based spice,
or just plain paprika, and a few sprigs of rosemary.

Cover it with foil, and roast it in a relatively hot
oven, say, 375 degrees for a medium-size bird, for one
and three-quarter hours or two hours if it seems to
require that. After the first hour, remove the foil for
it to brown.

Serve with a green salad and a great deal of red wine. This particular dish brings to mind the poem of René Char, just quoted, about cooking with love.

This recipe was inherited from a cousin, John Angel, who helped restore the cabanon:

Côtes d'Agneau Angel/
Lamb Chop Angel

Calling for a generous lamp chop per person, to be browned in a heavy saucepan in which two cloves of garlic have been sautéed in some sizzling butter. Turn once, and serve rare with lemon and herb butter, and a side dish of sautéed mushrooms, preferably *chanterelles.*

Malcolm's Gigot d'agneau/
Grilled Lamb,

for which he marinates a leg of lamb overnight, in his own red wine from last year, and freshly minced garlic, from the long string freshly purchased in the Carpentras market, with rosemary from his bushes and the greenest olive oil, and places it on the metal strips over the hot flame, just visible between the pale-colored stones.

He serves it with a *confiture d'oignons (onion preserve)* and some potatoes tossed in butter with a few cloves of garlic.

The many pictures of the very photogenic Malcolm in various publications, celebrating the remarkable feat of an Englishman making superb French wine on French soil with French grapes, were splendid. The newspapers would show his handsome face with his white moustache and the twinkling blue eyes over the rim of the wine glass he was raising in the clear air, its crimson contents showing to advantage against the backdrop of the greenery around and the purple mountain in the distance. The wine was indeed amazing: a rich nutty taste with such depth, you tasted the velvety flavor going through layer down to layer, still deeper.

One October evening, we wanted to celebrate the harvest, one year when we had all worked through it (me not very long, my fingers froze, I took too long to assort the grapes, but the sense of community was there). Janet prepared her famous

Gigot au miel/
Honeyed Leg of Lamb, with rice and raisins.

She has inserted into the lamb a few sprigs of rosemary and slivers of garlic, coated the meat with a fine dark honey, like that from the mountain chestnuts or thyme, and roasted it until is a perfect shade of dark pink.

She serves it with rice studded with golden raisins, and the thinnest green beans to be found. We all fall happily silent, over the carafes of new wine.

Mette's Agneau et Aubergine/
Lamb and Eggplant
from Les Cagarelles, Mormoiron

1kg of lean lamb (shoulder or leg), deboned and
  cut in chunks
250 grams of thinly sliced onions
4–5 large ripe tomatoes in slices or a tin of
  chopped tomatoes
4–6 large juicy cloves of garlic, minced
2–3 medium-sliced aubergines, neatly sliced
1½ tablespoons olive oil

salt, pepper, and provençal herbs, e.g. thyme and
perhaps a sprig of rosemary, or whatever you
find on the hillside; or basil if you have a pot on
your window sill.

Grease an oven-proof dish with olive oil and layer
the ingredients in the following order: the onion,
mixed with garlic and drizzled with oil; the lamb,
brushed with oil and sprinkled with herbs; the sliced
aubergine, drizzled rather more generously with oil;
the tomatoes, which should completely cover the
aubergines; salt and pepper and the rest of the oil
(add a little if you have run out). Sprinkle with more
herbs and salt and pepper before putting into a low
oven for about 4 hours

Serves six: I would serve this with pasta or rice
from the Camargue. Or I would use *épeautre*
(spelt); but I would serve no other vegetable
with it.

Gigot en Cocotte aux Olives/ Leg of Lamb with Olives
Adapted from Richard Olney's
A Provençal Table, *Pantheon Books, 1995*

In a *doux-feu* or other heavy cooking pot, warm 4 tablespoons of olive oil. (The *doux-feu* has the great advantage of not letting the meat dry out, since you put water in the indentation on the top.) Put in a six-pound seasoned leg of lamb and turn it over during a half hour, then add a chopped onion and stir until it turns golden. Add 2 heads of garlic (with the cloves peeled and crushed), two peeled tomatoes, a branch of thyme, and, to begin with, three table-spoons of white wine, cover the pot, and cook over very low heat for 2 hours. You add more wine every quarter of an hour, about a cup in all, and turn the lamb over frequently. Add five ounces of black olives Provençal style or Greek style. Before removing the pot, add four filets of anchovies, and discard the thyme.

Even reading the recipe, let alone preparing it, makes me happy.

Tata cannot drive, never having learned, depending entirely on her husband and sons to do the marketing: each bit of bread she has to ask for, each errand. Time was when the butcher and the baker and the grocer each came up the hill in a little truck, so she and the others here who do not drive could get their necessities . . . that time is no more. However, she is still much reputed, and deservedly, for her cooking, as well as her steadfast affections. Here's one of her favorite recipes:

Tata's Boeuf braisé provençale/ Braised Beef Provençal,

which calls for a piece of beef in pieces, or the cheaper kind especially for braising ("*le bec de loi*") or you can just ask for "*viande qui soit goûteuse en boeuf à la mode*" (meaning: that will be tasty fixed this way). You will need a half pound per person, corn or tomatoes, peeled and seeded, a *bouquet garni,* half a cup of dry white wine, half a cup of water, and some rice. Brown, in a mixture of half oil (not olive) and half butter. Surround it with carrots, small onions or shallots, and some tomatoes, peeled and with their seeds removed. Add a bouquet garni (thyme, bay leaf, celery, parsley), and enough liquid to cover: half a cup of dry white wine, and half a cup of water. You simmer it for two hours in a slow oven, and add stoned green olives just enough to heat them at the last moment.

Poulet marché/
Chicken Market Style

Ah, the chicken you can bring home from the market, where you see them roasting on the spit. Yellow ones, *poulet jaune,* or larger free-range, or *poulet de Bresse,* and so many other sorts. You can also just get a *cuisse* or thigh. I always take the juice and onions you can reheat if you aren't keeping them warm in the roasting paper. I serve whatever kind I get with ratatouille I make on top of the stove before I leave for the market: it won't burn in my *doux-feu* with the water I put in the oval slot on top. The orange one always cheers me up, as I've already said, but it is *very* heavy.

Poulet classique avec son ail, ses herbes, et ses olives/
Classic Chicken, with Garlic, Herbs, and Olives

I allow one chicken for two or three people, and decide whether or not to put a whole lemon in the cavity before I do anything else. Sometimes I use a *citron confit* or cooked lemon at the market, sometimes

René Char PHOTO JACQUES ROBERT.

René Char and Pablo Picasso, 1965, on the Ventoux

René Char with Matthew and Hilary, discussing lavender, at Les Busclats

Hilary with a friend

The yellow 2CV, outside the cabanon

Malcolm and Gerhard, with Malcolm's wine

Jean-Marie Conil at the cabanon

Augusta ("Tata") Conil, in her cherry trees

a fresh one. Then I place a little sliver or two of garlic and thyme or rosemary under the skin here and there, and brown the chicken in olive oil and garlic. Then I place it to roast over medium heat with a few stoned olives and three or four tomatoes. Serve with potatoes, tossed in olive oil and garlic, or with separately cooked onions and butter.

> I would probably serve this with a very simple dish of spinach, just boiling in a tiny bit of water very briefly, chopping it finely, tossing it in olive oil and garlic, and squeezing over it a bit of lemon.

Malcolm's Fegato à la Veneziana/Foie de veau à la Veneziana

Up the hill, Malcolm shows me how to make his calf liver, which is briefly sautéed in a pan over a large quantity of sliced onions that have been stirred about. Perhaps I was dreaming: I think that once he put a spoonful of that sweet Beaumes de Venise Muscat over it: what wouldn't this divine beverage lend its special taste to?

Even those unfortunate beings who are not wild about the taste of liver cannot resist this—nor should they. The key is the very brief cooking: it must retain at least some pink.

Lapin en Gelée au Basilic/
Rabbit in Basil Aspic
Philippe et Catherine Amiet, Cabanon Amiet

*A recipe from my neighbors in the cabanon next to mine
up the hill. It is bright with local color and ingredients:*

A rabbit (bought at the Pernes market, cut in
    pieces)
A good portion of streaky bacon, diced
Three cloves of garlic, sliced
Two yellow onions (bought from Claude, formerly a
    shepherd on the Mont Ventoux, from his place
    near the church in Mormoiron), cut in circles half
    an inch across
3 bay leaves, and a pinch of thyme, savory, a
    small stalk of rosemary (from the cabanon)
Coriander seeds
5 soup spoons of olive oil
½ a wine glass of Pastis (Pastis Henri Baroin, from
    Manosque, the village of Jean Giono)
A whole glass of dry white wine (Clairette, bought
    from the cave co-operative of Saint-Didier)
4 carrots, peeled and cut in circles
Salt (fleur de sel from the Salt Flats of southern
    France) and freshly ground pepper

⅓ liter of water

For the aspic, half of a calf's hoof or a packet of
   gel

The leaves of two branches of basil

Heat the olive oil and brown in it the pieces of
rabbit, the bacon, the garlic, and the onion. Set it all
aflame with the pastis and then wet it with the white
wine. After five minutes of cooking, add the bay
leaves, thyme, savory, rosemary, coriander, and the
calf's foot: mix it and cover with the carrots. Add the
water, salt, and pepper. Cook over medium fire for 45
minutes. At the very end of the cooking process, add
the rabbit's liver and let it cool.

When it is sufficiently cooked, remove the rosemary and the calf's foot. Debone the rabbit and discard the bones. Mix all the cooking ingredients,
adding the basil leaves. Place in a terrine and decorate the top with the bay leaves and carrots. Leave
in the refrigerator for two days. Serve cool, with a
green salad, and René Char's favorite wine, a red
Cairanne.

Christopher's Lapin à la sarriette/ Savory Rabbit

We all love it when Chris makes his rabbit: first he goes to find the savory in some neighboring field, before purchasing the rabbit itself, either in a market or at the butcher's.

This calls for a whole rabbit or chicken, or then one in pieces, to be shaken up with a little flour with salt and pepper, and browned slightly in a hot saucepan or casserole with garlic and butter, to which the savory (*sariette*) is added. He browns some mushrooms in butter on the side, and puts white or red wine in the pan: a half bottle for rabbit, which is very dry, and a fourth of a bottle for the chicken, less dry. Then he adds the meat, with the mushrooms. He bakes it an hour or so in a moderate oven until done.

Légumes
Vegetables

⁕⁗⁕

Tata's Artichauts—à la barigoule, mode d'ici/ Artichokes From Here

She uses about four small artichokes per person, about a potato per person, a few carrots, a branch of celery for each person, also a few small onions, three cloves of garlic, some olive oil, and a bouquet garni. She sets these tiny purple artichokes to boil, with the sliced potatoes, the carrots, celery, onions, and crushed garlic. Then she presses it down into the bottom of a pot called a "*cocotte*" in which there has been placed just a little bit of olive oil, "*un fond d'huile d'olive*." She adds a bouquet garni, enough water to cover, and cooks it an hour or so, until the water is absorbed. At the last minute, if she feels like it, she adds a few pitted black olives and a little olive oil.

Beverley in Caromb has the talent of inviting many people to dinner and doing it with great ease and simplicity. This is the ideal kind of dish to serve at such a time, permitting the cook to spend all her time with her guests.

Beverley's Asperges au Fromage/ Asparagus with Cheese

Break the ends off the asparagus, add a half cup of onions, toss the asparagus in a skillet with olive oil, and then run them under the broiler with a good quantity of parmesan cheese until the cheese turns brown.

And you can do the same thing with zucchini or yellow squash. Equally delicious, and equally easy.

Ann's Aubergines percées aux herbes/ Eggplant with Herbs

For dinner on her terrace, fragrant with the blossoms of the overhanging wisteria vine, and under the bright Provençal stars, Ann serves this.

Just some tiny eggplants, in whose skin you insert small sprigs of thyme and garlic, before rubbing with olive oil and grilling until the skin is charred.

Aubergine Paradis/
Eggplant Paradise

Slice a large unpeeled eggplant in rounds not too thick. (If you want to go through all that weighting and draining of them first, fine; if not, fine.) Have three bowls ready: in one, you put a cup of flour, with a good quantity of salt and pepper; in another, two beaten eggs and water, in the third, the bread crumbs (the Japanese kind, or panko, are best, but any will do, or make your own). You dip the eggplant slices in the flour mixture, then in the eggs, and then, of course, in the crumbs. Put them on a baking dish with a substantial drizzle of olive oil atop each one, some sprigs of thyme and rosemary, and some shavings of the best Parmigiano-Reggiano cheese, and bake in a hot oven (500 degrees) until the cheese turns brown.

Paradise indeed: the eggplant will be moist and crunchy, and the cheese runny. I like to serve this with sliced tomatoes and basil (can't have too many herbs), and as often, a bit of tapenade alongside.

N.B.: Some purists will have you choose between fresh herbs: actually, I would never give up my fresh basil from my necessary plant, nor, indeed, the tarragon from my salad, just because some other herb was sitting prettily atop my eggplant.

Tata tells me what to do with those heavy long vegetables I find only in France, called "blettes":

Tata's Blettes Provençales en Omelette/ Swiss Chard in Omelet

You parboil the whole long green top and the white bottom, then divide each stalk in two. The top you cut very finely and use in your omelet as if it were spinach, and the bottom you put to *sauter* with garlic and olive oil, either to serve alongside the omelet, or in it, mixed along with the green part. In either case, she said, you serve it with a tomato salad, so your plate will look red, yellow and green.

I don't find that these *blettes* have much taste any other way, so I'm very grateful to have something to do with them.

Brocoli Epicé/
Broccoli Hot

Toss a good amount of broccoli rabe, or cauliflower, into a pot of boiling water, and simmer it until done. Drain off the water, add red pepper flakes and enough olive oil and chopped garlic to season it well. I also like it with a few pitted black olives.

This is a perfect outside dish, if you want something hot in both senses. Or then late at night for a tasty and tasteful treat, which I always serve on a black oval platter.

Janet's Carottes rapées/
Janet's Carrots

Scrape or shred five or six large carrots into a mixing bowl. Please three tablespoons or even more of black mustard seeds in a saucepan in enough olive oil to cover the pan, and you will find them exploding after a moment.

Pour the mustard seeds, whatever oil remains, and some additional very fragrant olive oil over the raw carrots—this makes a splendid and remarkably simple dish, full of color and taste.

The olive oil from Malemort right up the hill from

Mormoiron is superb, as is that from Caromb, or then Les Baux, all very different. After a round of tasting, you know which is which instantly. There are thousands of terrific local olive oils; choose the one nearest you with the most flavor.

Concombres à la crème et fines herbes/ Cucumbers with Cream and Herbs

Peel the cucumbers, cut them in thin slices, and steam and season them. Carefully heat some *crème fraîche légère* in a saucepan, add the cucumbers and a heaping quantity of herbs (tarragon, basil, or just herbes de provence), and serve instantly.

This is a perfect accompaniment to any fish or roast.

Courgettes with Red Onions and Mushrooms

In slicing courgettes, Boyce always cuts them diagonally, rolling them along as he goes—to make small cones. Toss them in a pan with olive oil, garlic, whatever mushrooms you feel like serving that day, and cook until tender but not too well done. Sprinkle the juice of half a lemon over them before serving.

Beverley's Courgettes au Fromage/ Squash with Cheese

Thinly slice zucchini and onions, a cup of zucchini to a half cup of onions, toss them in a skillet with olive oil, and then run them under the broiler with a good quantity of parmesan cheese until the cheese turns brown.

And you can do the same thing with asparagus.

Mette's Tian de courgelles/ Tian of Squash
from Les Cagarelles, Mormoiron

Ingredients for four to six according to what else is to be served:

½ kg courgettes (zucchini squash)
½ kg ripe tomatoes (or a tin of chopped tomatoes)
6 cloves of garlic, chopped
6 tablespoons of grated parmesan or pecorino cheese
6 eggs
a generous handful of chopped basil (or parsley if this is easier to obtain)
salt, pepper, and nutmeg

Wash courgettes but do not peel. Cut into cubes and allow to sweat with a little salt. Add 3 tablespoons of olive oil and cook gently but do not let the courgettes turn mushy. Add the skinned and chopped tomatoes and the chopped garlic. Allow to simmer a little longer so as to thicken slightly before pouring into a greased gratin dish (the *tian* = a Provençal baking dish, cone-shaped) of the right size (for this quantity: about 20 centimeters in diameter). Whisk the eggs and blend them into the vegetable mixture together with the cheese, the basil and salt and pepper. Bake in the oven on setting 4 or 5 (about 190 degrees) until the eggs have set and the tian has risen and just begun to turn golden. It usually takes about 35 minutes for this quantity; but do watch it, as it is sad if the eggs get too set.

> You can serve this hot, lukewarm, or cold (excellent for picnics and al fresco lunches) and if you want it to be the main dish of your meal, you can add chopped cooked ham for the final stage.

I love having friends over to dinner, even more than eating alone with Colette. There is something especially satisfying about bringing out the heavy Le Creuset casseroles, those called "*doux-feu*" and containing some dish such as *poulet à l'estragon* or Tarragon Chicken or perhaps with rosemary from our own plants upstairs, or then a simple *porc aux pruneaux* or pork and prune dish. For dishes that take carving, such as the ones with chicken or lamb or rabbit, they rest on the wooden meat platter—the groove in the middle is worn down with years of use, perfect for catching all the liquid.

My simpler meat dishes I may serve with *riz au safran ou poivrons,* that is, rice with saffron or peppers, with a few chanterelle mushrooms if they are in season; or perhaps a pilaf with raisins, or then some just slightly burned garlic potatoes *pommes de terre à l'ail,* and a classic ratatouille. The more complicated ones taste better with some crunchy green beans, with butter and thyme: **Haricots verts au beurre et au thym/Green Beans with Butter and Thyme** from my thyme plant upstairs, that nestles along-side the rosemary bushes, cooked slowly for about an hour in a heavy iron casserole with a half cup of water, and served in the red ovenware pottery, with a ring or two of fresh onion over them.

Endives Extra/
Extraordinary Endives

Take off the outside leaves and the ends, and cut them longwise or in rounds. Dress them with good olive oil, lemon juice, and salt and pepper. This is a superb salad, and very beautiful alongside tomatoes, grilled or just sliced, with basil leaves on top.

Or then prepare them just that way, and broil them with a smattering of yellow cheese on top. Or do both: why not have a lunch of endive? Right now.

Haricots verts au citron, froids ou chauds/
Green Beans with Lemon, Hot or Cold

You boil some green beans until they are just crisp, not over four minutes, without letting them lose their greenness, pour off the water, and toss them in hot olive oil or butter to which a clove or two of chopped garlic has been added, or in which some shallots have been softened. Drizzle the juice of a fresh lemon over them, and rush them and yourself to the table. I like black olives tossed with them in the oil at the very last minute. You might throw in a tomato or two for added color.

THE CHICKPEA

Many of us have an abiding relation with the chickpea, in any combination whatsoever. I actually get them in the can, to save time, especially if non-family members are coming, but I can also see the advantage of the real thing. The chickpea is the emblem of simplicity, and it is nourishing:

Pois-chiches garnis à la mode de Provence/ Chickpeas Provençal Style

You soak them overnight with a pinch of bicarbonate of soda, rinse them, boil them with an onion and a couple of cloves, a sprig of thyme, a bay leaf, and a carrot for two hours, salting them at the end. Drain them and serve hot with olive oil, red wine or tarragon vinegar, salt, onions, pepper, and basil or parsley.

The last guest to whom I served this asked for three more helpings after the first: it is that kind of dish.

Anne's Poivrons farcis/
Stuffed Peppers,

which are medium sized red peppers, sliced in half lengthwise, with the seeds removed. Put the pepper halves into a well-oiled baking dish, and stuff each one with a peeled tomato and quite a few slivers of garlic.

Criss-cross the tomatoes with anchovy fillets and cover with sprigs of thyme. Season with freshly ground black pepper, and a little salt, and trickle some good fruity olive oil over the whole dish. Cover with foil, and bake in a moderate to hot oven until the peppers are tender (about an hour). Best served tepid, but good cold too.

Poivrons trois couleurs/
Tricolor Peppers

The simplest possible way of adding color to your dishes, whatever they are. I like to serve chicken, probably roasted, on a black plate with these peppers to the side, perhaps with some rice. Plunge yellow, green, and red peppers into a pot of boiling water, remove the seeds, and toss them briefly in a pan with olive oil (or butter if you prefer—for some reason that escapes me). They cheer up any meal and are especially good alongside mountain ham or *jambon cru*. Can be served hot or cold.

Coulis de tomates/
Tomato Coulis

Peel the tomatoes by plunging them into boiling water and then into cold water: the skins come off easily. Place them and some chicken broth into a pot to simmer until the mixture is thick and even. Add a few chopped onions to the brew, and add a few sprigs of tarragon or some fresh basil. You might feel, as I do, that tiny or modest fragments of the scallions I always have on hand are a help: colorful, flavorful, and a great addition of zip to many dishes.

Tomates et Fromage/
Cheese Tomatoes

Take some smallish-sized tomatoes, cut off the tops, and mix the scooped-out flesh with some relatively soft cheese (I have used all sorts, but the traditional cheese to use is Gruyère, which you melt with black and cayenne pepper, a clove of garlic crushed, and a dollop of mustard in a double saucepan with a splash of white wine). If you want to sacrifice the scooped-out flesh, you can use it for *gazpacho* or a *coulis de tomate*.

This mixture fills the tomatoes, which are then baked in the oven and broiled to blacken the tops. If you have vegetarian friends, this is perfect as the center dish for a lunch.

Tomates Provençales/
Provençal Tomatoes

Halve some very large tomatoes, preferably bought this morning in the market. Press a handful of chopped parsley, crushed garlic, salt, pepper, and, if you like, bread crumbs into the flesh, drizzle some olive oil over it, and broil until slightly blackened.

Pâtes, Pommes de Terre, et Riz
Pasta, Potatoes, and Rice, etc.

꧁꧂

Pommes de terre Cabanon/
Cabanon Potatoes

I use red-skinned potatoes, boil them slightly with
their skins on, and toss them in a pan with olive oil
and a lot of garlic, until they turn black and crunchy.

Another way I like serving potatoes, just as attractive as the
black and crunchy ones above, is:

Pommes de terre en Robe de champ,

which calls for four smallish potatoes per person, to
be washed and set for six or seven hours in an earthenware dish, on an asbestos pad on the stove, or then

on a charcoal or wood-burning fire. Check after a few hours, and turn them on their sides, adding more butter and parsley.

Paella

In my easy version, I toss two cloves of minced garlic and an onion in about a quarter cup of olive oil, and let them sizzle for a moment or two. Then I add cut-up leeks and carrots, some red and yellow pepper, a few rounds of whatever fiery sausage I can find, and whatever I might have around. I might have some shrimp or leftover chicken, and then I add a cup of rice to stir around until it is translucent, at which point I pour enough boiling chicken or fish stock over the rice to cover it all. I allow two and a half cups of liquid to a cup of rice. At the last minute, I add a few tiny freshly shelled peas, to make it *Paella valencienne.*

Often, friends from near or far would come to visit the cabanon, quite unlike a usual dwelling. I would generally toss together a late and light lunch, perhaps just some very ripe tomatoes and lettuce, liberally dosed with pinches from the basil plants, with a smidgen of sausage and cheese, accompanied by fresh bread. Or the delightful and easy-to-make hot potato salad, everyone's favorite dish, about which I can only say that the difference between it and that tasteless cold mayonnaise-soaked mush thing people used to serve on picnics is immense. Vast. This superbly simple dish is surely one of the main reasons for which, when we first arrive in Provence, we go toward a basil plant straight off, to have on hand all summer:

Pommes de terre en salade chaude/ Hot Potato Salad,

allowing at least three boiled potatoes per person, leaving the skins on, and being sure not to let them get mushy. Add a vinaigrette with the greenest olive oil you can find while the potatoes are still hot, lots of freshly ground pepper, and still more fresh basil.

I just put the plant on the table, or many generous sprigs in front of the bowl of hot potatoes, with salt from the Camargue and the Peugeot pepper mill I got from the Friday market in Carpentras. It came from the first stall up the main street of the market when you leave the peripheral highway around the Platanes parking lot, and a more useful purchase I cannot remember making. You can adjust the grind: I like it as coarse as possible, and these potatoes do too.

Matthew's favorite dish, no matter what the weather outside the cabanon, was this easy and comforting one, to be eaten anywhere at any time.

Pommes de terre croquantes/
Crunchy Potatoes

What is referred to in the French manuals as coming from "our ancestors the Gauls" comes in handy here: I'm sure they must have served the potatoes this way. In some old houses, there is a special place near the stove for a long roasting session of this kind.

Or then you can use red-skinned potatoes, boil them slightly with their skins on, and toss them in a pan with olive oil and a lot of garlic, which should turn black and crunchy. So do the potatoes, and you should always make many more than you think necessary.

Pommes de Terre en Diable/
Potatoes in a Pot

I put this recipe in to honor Roger Fry, who loved Provence, who imported French painting into England, and who transported the clay pot called a "diable" all around France on his bicycle, in order to cook Provençal style. You wash this strange and wonderful thing only once, the first time. That's it.

You scrub the potatoes, but without peeling them, and simply stick them in the *diable* for about an hour and fifteen minutes, in a moderate oven (350 F). No water, no nothing: it just works like a miracle.

Or then, you slice them, peel them, and, when they come hot out of the *diable,* you season them with olive oil and tarragon, salt, and pepper. You can always use basil if you don't have tarragon, but I love the taste of tarragon in salads of all kinds, as well as with chicken.

Taboulé

Perfect to take on expeditions up the Ventoux, or to the Lac du Paty, near Le Barroux, or anywhere else is the easily portable grain dish called Taboulé, best prepared for eating made the night before and chilled. The small grains are pale, and I like to give them color and taste with the mint picked from our field, freshly squeezed lemon juice and some of the lemon skin, with thin slices of red peppers and red onions, and black and green olives scattered through it, under the scattered sprigs of mint atop it.

It is also the dish of preference if you are just having a few friends or family members at home, because of its ease, its stretchability (you can add friends and family members up to the last minute, simply stirring in other ingredients at the last moment). The more, the better—it seems to work out that way.

Salades
Salads

❧

A good recipe for vinaigrette comes from up the hill, from Lucy, Malcolm and Janet's daughter, tall and elegant, with a kind of Renaissance beauty, blond hair, narrow face, and a sunny temperament—and this is a sunny temperament of a vinaigrette:

Lucy's Sauce Vinaigrette

calls for a pinch of salt, a spoonful of grainy mustard, a dribble of tarragon vinegar, a clove of crushed garlic, some green olive oil, and some pepper, freshly ground. (I have taken to growing my own tarragon, so I add a few sprigs of that.) Then you can add shallots or onions, the purple Simiane ones for color, and then some slices of bright red pepper, and fresh basil.

These potatoes remove anxiety completely and instantly.

This is exactly the kind of vinaigrette to use on the hot potato salad, on the chick peas you have saved half of from the **soupe aux pois chiches/chickpea soup**, or indeed any kind of salad, hot or cold.

It is also delicious on cold fish or meat. Or just about anything except dessert

Concombres Cabanon/
Cucumbers Cabanon Style

Get out your *mandoline,* and if you don't have one, and you like cucumbers thinly sliced, you peel them, slice them ahead of time, sprinkle salt over them, and put a weight on them to drain out the liquid. Later (wait at least 40 minutes), add some good olive oil, a bit of balsamic vinegar, and some chives or/and Italian or French parsley.

This is magnificent with any roast or fish.

Endive, Fromage bleu, Radicchio/ Endive, Blue Cheese, and Radicchio

My favorite cheese for this one is Fourme d'Ambert, blue with with a special taste. You can also use any Danish blue cheese or then an Italian Gorgonzola: this salad is so good that any kind of blue cheese will work well.

The red of the radicchio and the white endive and the blue of the cheese make a delightful combination of colors. Then you add a half cup of walnut pieces and your favorite vinaigrette and serve, preferably at a lunch outside under some trees.

L'heure du Thé
Teatime

✿

For tea, I would often make the easiest of all concoctions to
be baked, which I first had years before in Brittany, visiting
my friend Monique Chefdor, a specialist in the writing of
the poet Blaise Cendrars. She would make it in the afternoon, any time it was raining, just the way my mother would
long for a gingerbread in the South in that kind of weather.

Quatre-quarts/
Four-fourths

just takes four eggs, a cup of butter, a cup of flour, a
tiny bit of baking powder, and a cup of sugar—
everything has the same quantity here. You cream
the eggs with the butter, add the sugar and when it
is thoroughly mixed, add the flour, and cook in a
moderate oven for an hour.

Nothing could be more useful or more aesthetic;
you can spoon rum over the Quatre-quarts. . . .

Les Desserts
Desserts

❧❧❧

Bananes les plus belles

Once, in a market in St. Germain-en-Laye, right outside Paris, home of Maurice Denis and other sym-
bolists, I found an immense black saucepan, perfect
for serving six or more people. In this I would make
caramelized bananas, easy and impressive. I would
just remove the peels and toss the bananas with
butter and sugar until they caramelized, and add a
quantity of dark rum. Then I would serve them with
a light *crème fraîche*.

FRUITS ROUGES, FRUITS VERTS/FRUITS RED AND GREEN
All these desserts look like Impressionist still lifes and taste like the living thing. I am especially fond of

Figues et fromage blanc/
Figs and White Cheese.

Here, the purple green of the figs (well, I do have a fig tree, and they are greenish-purple, and I pick them the first thing in the morning before the ants get to them. . . .). In any case, the color of the figs and the white of the cheese set each other off to perfection, sugared or not, cut up or whole. If you happen to have some green almonds available, put a little dish of them alongside, and let each person remove the kernels while eating. The combination is unbeatable.

Janet's Abricots au Four/
Baked Apricots

In the Vaucluse, up by Le Barroux, it is the custom to alternate olive trees with apricot bushes, so that the dull green and the orange make an aesthetic pattern.

Janet puts a heap of golden apricots in an earthenware dish and pours over them a heavy *crème fraîche* or a *crème fluide,* sprinkles them with lemon juice and sugar, and bakes them in a slow oven until they wrinkle just slightly. At the table, everyone adds a dash of Grand Marnier from the bottle on the table. A dessert fit for the gods.

My favorite dessert is one I prepare in my gigantic skillet from St. Germain-en-Laye, just outside Paris, some fruit tossed in fresh butter and calvados for dessert, like:

Bananes au caramel/ Caramel Bananas;

that is, bananas just cooked to brownness in a sauce made of brown sugar melted with butter and flamed with rum at the last moment. I have bought some *crème fraîche,* to put in dollops on the dish—it melts invitingly over the rum, and everyone has more than one helping. I put on a cassette of Monteverdi, and everyone falls silent.

When I serve this dessert, it is always late at night, or very early morning. My friends I will have served it to, all usually in very good temper, will depart in those early hours by the path of highly irregular stones leading down to the narrow road. They may catch their loose clothing in the branches or the brambles, along that way rather sparsely lit here and there by little oval lights in the bushes that look as if they should be lighting the deck of a ship. When they arrive in the road below, by the tomato patch, there may be a few cars coming up or down. In the daytime, there are more likely to be motorbikes or sturdy walkers, ready for the climb uphill. But as the dark falls, the atmosphere changes, and the place grows silent. Perhaps you can just hear some faint fall of a twig in the wind. Most often, though, it is peaceful, among the trees, and happily, I tend to forget, in such a mellow mood, the many smallnesses of a Provençal village. They are in any case balanced by the collective joys, such as dinners shared under the overwhelming stars.

Cerises a l'eau de vie/ Cherries with Alcohol
Preserved for the future

Into the pile of cherry mush, I put some cloves and lots of sugar, feeling highly accomplishful. Some *Burlats* do not have a strong enough flavor for such preparation, and the white *napoléon* have no taste at all, but I have mostly *coeur-de-pigeons.* I never bother to label anything, so that years from now, we will still be having surprises, good and bad. With the cloves and a bit of vanilla bean, any cherries look like something dark and wonderful. I serve them sometimes for tea, perhaps, on the crisp and almost tasteless rectangular biscuits made by Lu, that come wrapped in separate tinfoil packages. Or make them into a *coulis* for my *quatre-quarts*. Sometimes after dinners here, I serve the cherries from years and years ago—dark and small and fierce-aromaed.

Crème Caramel au Cabanon/ Cabanon Custard

I am putting this in as my daughter Hilary's favorite dessert. It is also an easy delight to make, even if the oven doesn't always work properly—it is good even if it is runny—just do not overcook it.

You beat four eggs, whole, with a liter (or quart, it doesn't matter too much) of whole milk and a cup of sugar. Then you flavor the superbly simple mixture with vanilla (yes, I use artificial as happily as the Real Thing) and a bit of almond flavor if you like. Grate fresh nutmeg over it, and place the bowl in a pan of water, enough to reach about a third of the way up the bowl. Bake for about an hour, in a moderate oven. Try it, and if it is not the way you like it, continue baking. (Not so long that the top cracks, though.)

Coulis de Framboise/
Raspberry Coulis

One of my family's favorite desserts for lunch was always one of the simplest, combining cheese and fruit and sweetness. It is a perfect combination for what we all here, believers or not, call God's country. It is just a soft white cheese with cream and raspberry sauce made in a blender.

Crême brûlée/
Burnt Cream, and a Tip for the Top

You beat four egg yolks, place them in a smallish heavy casserole, add a cup of heavy cream, and stir constantly over heat until the mixture coats the spoon. Set to cool in ramekins, or in a glass bowl, and place over the top a thick coating of brown sugar before you run it under the broiler. I take the easy way and first draw the outline of the dish upon some foil, and put that circle of sugar on tinfoil under the broiler to harden it, so it just fits atop the chilled crème. Very simple, and leaves the egg whites free to make into a simple meringue.

Meringue Simplicissimus,

for which you beat those egg whites stiff (three or four), beat in a cup of sugar (cristallisé, one-third at a time). Then you add one-third of a cup of confectioner's sugar (sucre glacé) and continue to beat, making sure the egg whites still stand up stiffly. Then bake on tinfoil, so they won't stick, for about forty-five minutes, and leave in the stove for two hours. They are good with anything, with sherbet or fruit atop, or just as a light crunchy treat to have with any dessert.

> N.B.: If I can make these things in a cabanon, easy as pie, anybody can make them anywhere, with very little effort.

Fruits rouges au froid/
Fruits Cold and Crimson,

for which you use any of these fruits in any proportion that is convenient: raspberries, strawberries, plums or *brugnons,* in pieces or slices, over which you put a good amount of sugar, letting them chill all day in a glass bowl, before squeezing over it all a fresh lemon and a sprig of fresh mint.

Janet's Mousse au chocolat/ Chocolate Mousse

To make this extraordinary concoction, Janet melts two bars of bitter or bittersweet chocolate in a double boiler or "*bain-marie*," adds the yolks of four eggs, then beats the whites until stiff but not dry, and adds them to the previous mixture which has been taken off the stove. Before it sets, she adds some Cointreau or Grand Marnier.

In one variant, the juice of a Seville orange is added, making it **Mousse au chocolat et à l'orange/Chocolate Orange Mousse. . . .**

When I walk back to my cabanon after such a dessert, I find myself humming something I can't identify—I must have heard it long ago somewhere. Then I sit outside under the stars, listen to the night noises—it might be one of those times the nightingale signals his presence—and think about getting up early. No rush, though.

Melons

Here in the corner by the steps is what I think of as a melon stone, one of the highly prized *pierres plates* Char gave us, the flat stones that are used to make patios and line walkways. My favorite melons are those I bring home from the tiny local market on Sunday morning, three for five euros, choosing the ripest and the heaviest. If they are too rounded to rest on the stone, I put them on the metal boot scraper outside the kitchen door to absorb the flavor of the sun, piling them up upon each other in a threesome. If they are not large enough and threaten to drop through, I use a thin stick on the old piece of metal and prop them there against the stone wall

Oranges au Vin rouge/ Oranges in Red Wine

Take a quantity of oranges, about twice what you would think you would be serving. Slice them thinly, put them in some table wine, from the cooperative you live near, if you are lucky. Otherwise, just about any light red wine will do. Add quite a bit of sugar, a bit more than you think necessary, and the slices. Refrigerate this for a few hours—it has to be really cold. Serve in white or glass dishes, with some simple cookies.

This may be the cabanon's favorite easily fixed dessert; it certainly is mine.

Pêches au Muscat/ Peaches in Muscat

A perfect dish if you have just been to the market and purchased a plateau de pêches, either yellow or white.

Simply slice the peaches and place them in shallow bowls with the best *Beaumes-de-Venise* you can find over them. I prefer to chill them, and sometimes sprinkle shaved almonds on top.

As you will have read, we far prefer the Beaumes-de-Venise from the Domaine de Durban, way at the top of a hill just outside of the town. It keeps and mellows to a deep golden color, improving every year.

Poires au Vin/
Pears in Wine

Pick the nicest-shaped pears you can find, and peel them. Boring but better.

Set them to boil in a pot with cinnamon sticks added to the water, and a great deal of sugar. When the pears are almost done, just about softened to the fork, remove them, and reduce the water to a thick sugary syrup. Remove the cinnamon sticks and chill the peeled pears in the syrup, standing on their ends.

A bit more complicated than the Oranges au Vin, but very beautiful. If you have some dessert plates you especially like, this is the time to use them, even in the cabanon.

VARIOUS IDEAS

❧

Ovens, Cooking, and Cooking Tools

I usually just say to myself: slow oven (French gas 2–4, US 200–300), my pressure cooker or my French Fry cutter, and often forget I have a blender. And so I am tempted just to put "slow" oven, or "bake a long time," knowing the reader of such a book will have private reasons for heat and time.

When I am back in America, and have a Provençal longing, I just substitute dried for fresh in herbs, and thinking of the olive oil from Les Baux, alternate between Colavita and the more recondite varieties—in any case, I like to use a lot, and have a Scotch upbringing, as the French seem to.

For any time at all, I put on any table one of the

brightest Provençal cloths I picked up in Carpentras or L'Isle or Bédoin, gather around some friends, and have a tiny glass of the Beaumes-de-Venise I brought back from the Domaine de Durban. I like the ones in blue and yellow, with blue olives.

Little by little, I acquired what I see as the basic cabanon cooking tools: a wire basket to shake the salad out of the door in, an asbestos pad to keep cooking from burning, a wire whisk to keep lumps out of the soup or anything else, a mortar and pestle for the pesto and for mashing garlic on all occasions, a steamer for vegetables, a wooden pepper mill for particularly coarse grind, with the workings made by Peugeot, a long ham knife, thin and razor-sharp, for making the thinnest slices of mountain ham, and a few heavy casseroles of iron covered with enamel. I like Le Creuset's orangish-red, and their *doux-feu,* a sort of Dutch oven with an oval scooped out on top where you put water in to drip down and keep things moist. It is like some miracle: nothing ever dries out, even when you leave it for hours. When the Quimo stores existed, a few years ago, I bought a few bright yellow plates to stand against the back of my very old kitchen *meuble* (they are now found in the basement of department stores, Galeries Lafayette for instance).

ON HERBS

It is nicest to pick the herbs you will be cooking with: sarriette for rabbit or chicken, from a little field, down some road, at the foot of some hills; rosemary for lamb, thyme for chicken, fennel for fish, from a bush found on your own or some neighbor's land. You have to get your basil plant fresh every season, but if you plant it and pick it at the top ("nipping" or "pinching"), and water it every day, it may last the season. In the markets, you can of course get everything, and the dried Herbes de Provence no home in any country should be without. You might want to use some sage for chickpeas, unless you like sarriette in them, but that is really all you need.

USEFUL TO HAVE ON HAND

caramel liquide: wonderful for putting on cake or over *crème fraîche* and any fruit, instant happiness for custard or milk.

chips (not the "anything with chips" English kind, but potato chips): get the "artisanal" kind if you can, irregular, salty, fresh and full of snap. These can be toasted and served with meat. Or dipped into your *anchoiade* or *caviar d'aubergines.*

citron confit: a whole preserved lemon, perfect for putting inside a roasting chicken or duck, or indeed anything you want to stuff for flavor.

coulis de. . .: a wonderful name for various sauces that can be smooth or irregular, depending on your taste. I give here recipes for *coulis de tomates* and *coulis de fraise ou framboise,* in the understanding that you can use the technique with a number of things. But easily available in a bottle is *coulis de framboise* (raspberry sauce). Wonderful for putting over any dessert, especially *fromage blanc* or *à la faisselle.*

crème fraîche: available in many varieties, depending on use (thicker or thinner, more or less delicate, more or less expensive) and addable to many things—over fruit or white cheese (either *fromage blanc* or the dense little rolls surrounded by thin paper, called *petits suisses*), or to make the Norman variety of *moules marinières,* to thicken soups or anything else.

fougasse: the traditional Provençal bread made with olive oil, which I like studded with cracklings or *lardons,* or then black olives. Serve very hot, preferably a little burned and crunchy. Don't leave the market without some.

fromage blanc: useful in dips, and to serve just so with *crème fraîche* on it on a hot day, with perhaps some sugar or a *coulis de framboise* or *de fraise*, raspberry or strawberry sauce. (Just squash the berries in some sugar, add some liqueur if you like. I like a lot.)

fromages: a plate of them, usually a goat cheese, maybe a *chèvre* with *cendres* or ashes around it, or herbs, a *bleu d'Auvergne* or *de Causse*, for color, that strange orangish Mimolette, a slice of aged *Cantal*, and some kind of *Brie*.

fruits à l'eau-de-vie: these are the cherries you picked years ago and put away in alcohol and serve now fifteen years or so later, with good friends and after a good meal.

grès: in this pale grayish-brown pottery, everything looks wonderful. I would put some black and green olives and tomatoes sprinkled with basil from the basil plant I faithfully water very day, with some country *paté*, a bunch of radishes and butter alongside, and a little bowl of mayonnaise and mustard and *baies roses*—those little red peppers that are sweet and crunchy—in the center of the table.

huile d'olive: some olive oil with spices, for fish, for example. You get it in the markets, all fiery red with peppers, and make a tiny nick in the cork at the top, for pouring out drop by drop. And then refill it as the need strikes you. You might want to use it up within two years, though.

If you like, as I do, very green and fruity olive oil, it is best of all to get it at the *moulin à huile* in one of the villages all around the countryside, for example in Entrechaux, near the Lac du Paty, or in Caromb. If you don't like it very fruity, you can refill your own bottle from one of the specialty stores in any town, or just get ordinary olive oil. A celebrated one is from Les Baux, available in Maussane-les-Alpilles, or by ordering from a specialty store. Fortunate it is to have a neighboring oil mill, from which you choose the variety you want, from very thick and green, to less thick and less green. I take my tin can and refill it from the next to thickest variety; all good olive oil has the remarkable property of perfecting whatever simplest things you have: the most ordinary lettuce (just "*salade*" or the crunchy "*croquante,*" or the curly-headed "*frisée*"), a few slices of tomato with basil and freshly ground pepper, or your lentil salad become a repast for the gods. And you and your friends.

There are wonderful olive oils available in French markets, which are marinated with red pepper and white peppercorns for fish, and other spices for other dishes. These run on the same principle as Balsamic vinegar, which you can use to good cheer on grilled meat as well as salad, and as special effect as you use raspberry vinegar. The stores in Provence, expensive but beautiful, called La Taste, specialize in these, and in most of them you can refresh your can of olive oil also, but the oil tends to be not very risky, not very frisky, not very green. It seems to be for tourists of the aesthetic, rather than for the hearty-appetited Provençal.

olives: you want at least three kinds, a spicy black one, with red pepper Moroccan style, or heavily garlic-scented. Perhaps then some calmer ones, tiny and tasty, like the black ones from Nice or Nyons (expensive), and some green ones if they have deep taste. Why not add some light brownish-green ones, flavored with lemon or herbs? The markets have all sorts, and the more sorts the better. I like to serve them in different-colored earthenware bowls, black and yellow and green and grès-colored.

miel: in the markets, there are more varieties of honey than you can try, from the pale "*toutes fleurs*" and the lavender to the dark throaty honeys from the top of the mountains (or the just plain "*miel de montagne*" so modestly titled). It is nice to have little pots of various types for guests, but once you hit on one you really like for yourself—"*miel de thym,*" for example, from thyme, or, in my case, the "*miel de châtaigner*" from chestnut trees—you may be hooked.

quatre-quarts: that Breton cake made with butter, flour, and sugar (recipe above). Great served with chunks (more fun than slices) of fresh yellow and white peaches just peeled, mixing their colors, especially if you pour over them a glass of dark rum and a bit of brown sugar, and top it with *crème fraîche* and *fromage blanc* mixed. A dessert for special friends. I hate to say you can buy it by the long loaf, very inexpensive, but you can, AND it keeps, AND it is good to have around for drop-ins.

riz: I prefer Uncle Ben's rice because it does not stick. But there are those who can use something else. *Charleston* is not bad. But *Taureau ailé* always sticks, in my experience.

saucisses: my favorite is filled with hazelnuts, or *noisettes,* or encased in *herbes de provence* or black pepper. Pretty good with anything mixed into them: olives, green pepper (*poivre vert*), and so on.

les tartines: the next morning when you want to use your French bread, you put a few drops of water on all its sides and bake it for a few minutes until it comes out crunchy on the outside and soft inside. Serve with mountain honey, or a large pot of raspberry jam *(confiture de framboise)* or apricot preserves *(confiture d'abricots)*.

Little Note on Varieties of Things: many things like choco-late, butter, *crème fraiche*, and so on, come in ordinary form ("*de ménage*") or for baking, and more delicate form, con-sequently more expensive. (Except for truly bitter choco-late, to have with Beaumes-de-Venise, for example, I generally get the least expensive kind. But that is up to your palate, your budget, and your general system of things.)

LES APÉRITIFS

un kir: put some good *crème de cassis* (the liqueur, not the sweet syrup for children's drinks) in some at least pretty good white wine—it should be rather pink, not palish like a California zinfandel.

un martini blanc ou rouge: these sweet vermouths, white and red, are very sweet indeed, the red seeming much sweeter than a Cinzano. The white is popular in Provence: my neighbor loves it.

Vermouth blanc, Boissière, or Chambéry: red or white. I prefer the white, which is rather like Lillet, with a fresh biting taste of herbs.

un panaché (a shandy, in England): beer and lemonade in equal quantities; anyone with a childish streak will love it in the form of a Monaco, tall and pink and fizzy.

des sirops (syrups): for children and abstaining grownups, in wonderful flavors—cerise (cherry) and grenadine for pink color, "menthe" (mint) for green, "pippermint" for blue, pamplemousse (grapefruit) or citron (lemon) for yellow, orgeat for cloudy white, or even anise (licorice, like Pastis).

jus de fruit au rhum: ananas, for example, pineapple with rum—or in your blender, to be served frothy.

And always **un pastis** (the licorice-flavored white very alcoholic delight): to serve at the drop of a straw hat, to anyone coming, with a little bowl of ice cubes and a jug of cold water, in long glasses, with olives or *tapenade*. You might want to stick to the good varieties such as 51, Ricart, and Casanis. (I served another brand recently, and there was much comment, kindly but firm, from the neighbors to whom I served it. Of course, you may have some friends who find it in odd places, or, better still, make it.) You put it in before the ice, and before you add more than that amount of water again, you will want to ask. The color should be a comforting yellow and cloudy; when it gets pale, dispositions suffer. Be sure to insist on your guests having more than one glass; otherwise, they will leave "limping."

homemade liqueurs: of various sorts; for example, juniper or some other aromatic plant.

Mireille's recipe: place a few sprigs of some highly potent plant with some sugar and eau-de-vie to marinate for 3 or 4 months; like *cerises à l'eau-de-vie*, it may profit by being placed in the sun for 3 or so weeks, and then kept in the dark. Serve coolish, preferably under some plane trees.

vin à l'orange (orange wine): place some red wine with orange peel in a saucepan to come just to a boil; marinate for a few months in a cool place, and serve with semi-sweet biscuits to good friends.

SOME QUICK NOTES ON WINE

❧

Needless to say, the best thing is to have a neighbor who makes superb wine. Many of the cooperatives in the little villages, as here in the Ventoux, have a perfectly good ordinary wine you get in liter bottles and then take them back for refilling when you need more. The rosés vary widely: there is a heavier Tavel, or a Lirac, which are of medium quality, and the rosé of Gigondas which is quite heavy. For the white wines, in fact, there is a very good Cairanne and also a Fondrêche in the vicinity (people here sometimes resort to Sylvaner and to the wines of Alsace for white, or, with their shellfish, Muscadet or Gros Plant of Brittany, or Sancerre for other dishes).

You can drive up in the hills to Beaumes-de-Venise for another good red wine, but it is famous above all for the delicate fragrance of the muscat golden wine to be served with foie gras, or put in melon halves for best occasions, or drunk in little glasses with dessert. The Domaine de Durban, right at the top of an interminable hill after a no less interminable woods gives you a sublime experience, not to be missed.

Further on are Vacqueyras, Cairanne, and Gigondas with their famous vintages, and Chateauneuf-du-Pape, with a great sea of wines, much of which is mediocre but among which is to be found some of the great wines of France. You might want to stay in a small hotel, as I did, in Vacqueyras, for example, near the Dentelles de Mont-mirail you can climb in the early morning, or in the late afternoon when the heat has abated a little, taking a good walking stick, a hat, and a book to rest with on the rocks at the top before going down to have a peaceful cup of coffee or aperitif at a stone table in a courtyard looking up at where you have been.

A WINE-TASTING

We go winetasting one day. You sniff, you swirl it about, you sort of crunch it in your mouth and you spit in the *crachoir,* or then on the floor or outside, depending on the place. We taste the wines in order of their bigness, more modest first, working up to the great ones. The ones here where we are tasting today have to be called Cotes du Rhône, because they aren't strictly speaking in the Vacqueras region. The grapes are Grenache, Syrah, and either Mouvèdre or Cinsault.

The *crachoir* where you spit out the swallow after sniffing it and twirling it in the glass and then swooshing it about in your mouth is too high for me to reach: I stand on tiptoe, exhausting, and finally decide just to swallow what I taste. After the plain "Cotes du Rhône," we try Signature 2003/4, then Geneste 2000 and 2003, and finally, the very grand Hautes Terrasses with only Syrah. Ah, what to say?

This kind of tasting is repeated in every vineyard we love here. May it always be this way!

Moun Pais
A mis ami de Mourmeiroun

Tout repauso, tout dor: lou gribet sout l'erbeto,
L'enfant dins sa bressolo e l'aucèu dins soun nis.
Iéu, soulet, dorme pas dins ma pauro chambreto,
      E pantaie moun bèu païs.

Se sabias coume es dur de quita lou vilage

. . .

Tambèn, la niue, lou jour, me desole, pecaire!
      E pantaie moun bèu païs.

Mourmeiroun! Mourmeiroun! Es pèr tu que souspire,
Es pèr tu que toujour moun cor tabassara.
La vido, luen de tu, me sara que martire
E jamai loui bonur à mis iue lusira.
      Oh! que sariéu urous se poudiéu lou revèire,
      Ma maire, mi parènt mis ami, moun bèu nis!
      Sarié tant de bonur que pode pas lou crèire
        E pantaie moun bèu païs.

From a Collection of Provençal Songs, 1870
Alphonse Michel, Extrait de "Lou Flasquet de Mestre
Miqueu, "*Recuei di Consoun Prouvençalo,*" 1870

My Country

To My Friends of Mormoiron

All is at rest, everything sleeps: the cricket in the grass,
The child in his cradle and the old one in his home.
I, all alone, am not asleep in my poor little room,
      And I am longing for my lovely country.

If you knew how hard it is to leave your village . . .

. . .

So night and day I am sorrowing, alas!
      And I am longing for my lovely country.

Mormoiron! Mormoiron! It's for you I am sighing,
It's for you that my heart will always be beating.
Life, far from you, is martyrdom for me
And no shine of happiness in my eyes.
Oh! how joyous I'd be if I could see you again,
My mother, my family, my friends, my lovely home!
I'd be too happy to believe it
      And I am longing for my lovely country.

EPILOGUE

Elizabeth David got it right, as so often it happens:

> Provence is a country to which I am always returning, next week, next year, any day now, as soon as I can get on to a train. . . . Now and again the vision of golden tiles on a round southern roof, or of some warm, stony, herb-scented hillside will rise out of my kitchen pots with the smell of a piece of orange peel scenting a beef stew. . . . What it amounts to is that it [the food of Provence] is the rational, right and proper food for human beings to eat.
>
> —*French Provincial Cooking*